LION

A Long Way Home

YOUNG READERS' EDITION

SAROO BRIERLEY

with Larry Buttrose

LION
A Long Way Home

YOUNG READERS' EDITION

Edited by Nan McNab

PUFFIN BOOKS

PUFFIN BOOKS
An imprint of Penguin Random House LLC
375 Hudson Street
New York, New York 10014

First published in Australia by Penguin Group (Australia), 2013
This young readers' edition published by Puffin Books,
an imprint of Penguin Random House LLC, 2017

Cover design by Tony Palmer © Penguin Random House Australia Pty Ltd
Text design by Penguin Random House Australia Pty Ltd
Images courtesy of the author, except where otherwise indicated
Typeset in Minion by Penguin Random House Australia Pty Ltd

LIBRARY OF CONGRESS CATALOGING-IN-PUBLICATION DATA IS AVAILABLE.

Puffin Books ISBN 9780425291764

Printed in the United States of America

5 7 9 10 8 6

For Guddu

Foreword

Imagine being totally lost as a tiny child. It amazes me now when I think about how I managed to survive and then thrive. When I was on the streets, so hungry and alone, I wondered what would happen to me. Would I be okay? I was by myself every day, even though I was among thousands of people. I truly had to trust and rely on my instincts. When I was taken to Liluah Home it was almost a relief because I didn't have to face the fear of the unknown.

When I was given the option of accepting a new family, I had real hope for my future – I thought that maybe I would be loved and cared for again. The idea that complete strangers would want to look after me as their own son was a concept I could hardly believe. I am so glad I accepted the opportunity to become part of a family again, and to begin my new life.

I wrote this book to show how powerful you can be

if you put your mind to it and use every resource and opportunity available. I went from a child without the benefit of education to a strong and healthy guy who wrote a book – WOW! I hope that my story will bring enlightenment to you on many levels.

I am truly thankful to my first mother who gave me the survival skills that saved my life on the streets of Kolkata and also to my new parents for giving me a new life in Tasmania.

We are all enjoying the excitement of making a film and sharing our story around the world.

Life is good.

Saroo Brierley

Contents

PROLOGUE

I lay in an unbelievably soft bed – my own bed – and gazed around the room. I'd never had a bedroom of my own before. For most of my five or six years I'd slept in a small room with my family, then later I'd slept in a dormitory with lots of other children. The only time I'd slept alone was when I lived on the streets of Calcutta.

I looked across at the wardrobe where I'd been shown my new clothes, warm ones for the Tasmanian climate. On the floor were boxes of picture books and toys. I still couldn't believe they were for me, and that I could look at them and play with them as I pleased. I half-expected some bigger kid to come along and take them. I still wasn't used to the idea of being safe, let alone having things of my own.

I was afraid of the dark, so my bedroom door was left open and a wedge of light from the hall shone on the floor – bright electric light, not a candle or kerosene lamp. On one wall of my bedroom was a big coloured picture with lots of strange writing on it: a map. One day, I would understand what a map was, and realise that it held the secrets of my past: where I'd come from, who I was, and who I'd left behind. But for now, I was too tired to care. I closed my eyes and slept.

1
Remembering

I had a map of India on my bedroom wall when I was growing up in Hobart. Mum – my new mother – had put it there to help me feel at home. But when I arrived in Tasmania, I didn't even know what a map was, let alone the shape of India. I had never been to school, I couldn't read or write or speak English. It was 1987, and they told me I was six years old. I didn't know for certain how old I was. On my official documents my birthday was 22 May 1981, but that was a guess by the Indian authorities, based on the day I had arrived at the orphanage, an ignorant, confused, lost little boy; they had guessed my age and my birth year, which I have never changed. I hadn't been able to explain much about who I was or where I'd come from. The first time I ever heard the name Calcutta was when my new mum and dad pointed to it on my map and told me that's where I came from. But they were wrong. I didn't come from Calcutta, but from somewhere much further away, and the story of how I got there was incredible.

At first, Mum and Dad didn't know how I'd become lost. All they knew – all anyone knew – was that I'd been picked off the streets of Calcutta and after attempts to find my family had failed I had been taken to the orphanage and then put up for adoption. Happily for all of us, I was adopted by the Brierleys.

Mum had decorated the house with Indian ornaments – Hindu statues, brass ornaments and bells, and lots of little elephant figurines. She had spread some Indian printed fabric across the dresser in my room, and placed a carved wooden puppet in a brightly coloured outfit nearby. All these things were sort of familiar, even if I hadn't seen anything exactly like them before. I had no idea that they were unusual objects to have in an Australian house.

At first, Mum didn't concentrate on teaching me English. It was far more important to comfort and care for me, and gain my trust, and you don't need words for that. She knew an Indian couple in the neighbourhood, Saleen and Jacob, and we would visit them regularly to eat Indian food together. They spoke with me in my own language, Hindi, asking simple questions and translating instructions and anything Mum and Dad wanted me to know about how we'd live our life together. Coming from a very simple background, I didn't speak much Hindi either, but being able to understand and be understood helped me settle in to my new home and family. If my new parents weren't able to communicate through gestures and smiles, Saleen and Jacob were always there to help.

Mum and Dad were very affectionate, right from the start, always giving me lots of cuddles and helping me to feel safe, secure, loved and, above all, *wanted*. That meant a lot to a child who'd been lost and had experienced what it was like when no one cared about him. Very soon I trusted them completely, and a strong bond grew between us. Even at the age of six, I understood that I had been given a rare second chance. I quickly became Saroo Brierley.

As children do, I picked up my new language quite quickly. But at first I spoke very little about my past in India. My parents didn't want to push me to talk about it until I was ready, and apparently I didn't seem to give it much thought. Mum remembers a time when I was seven, when out of the blue I became very distressed and cried out, 'Me begot!' ('I forgot!)

Later, she found out I was upset that I had forgotten the way to the school near my Indian home, where I used to walk to watch the students. We agreed then that it probably didn't matter anymore, but deep down, it did matter to me. My memories were all I had of my past, and privately I thought about them over and over, trying to ensure I didn't 'beget'.

In fact, the past was never far from my mind. At night, memories would flash by and I'd have trouble calming myself so I could sleep. Daytime was generally better, with lots of activity to distract me, but my mind was always busy. I was determined not to forget a single thing about my family, my home, or the fateful night I was lost. Some of these memories were good, and some of them bad – but I couldn't have one without the other, and I wasn't prepared to let a single one go. And so most of my childhood experiences in India remained in my memory as an almost complete picture – clear and fresh, and sometimes in great detail.

Safe and secure in my new home in Hobart, I thought perhaps it was somehow wrong to spend so much time thinking about the past – that my new life might need me to keep the old life locked away – so I kept my night-thoughts to myself. At first, I didn't have the language to speak about the past anyway.

More than anything I wanted to find my mother again, but once I realised that was impossible, I knew I had to do whatever it took to survive, so that one day I might be able to try and find her.

Occasionally the night-thoughts would spill over into the day. I remember Mum and Dad taking me to see the Hindi film *Salaam Bombay*. Its images of a little boy trying to survive alone in a sprawling city, in the hope of returning to his mother, brought back disturbing memories so sharply that I wept in the dark cinema, my well-meaning parents unaware of the cause.

Sad music of any kind, particularly classical music, could stir my emotions and my memories. Seeing or hearing babies cry also affected me strongly. But somehow the thing that stirred me up the most was seeing other families with lots of children. I suppose they reminded me of what I'd lost, even though I was aware of my good fortune.

I adapted to my country and culture fairly easily, most likely because I understood I was far better off in Australia than in India. Other adoptive parents might have hoped that I was young enough to forget, so I could start life afresh in Australia. But my mother and father had chosen to adopt a child from India for a reason. They did not want to wipe away my past or ignore my culture. Instead they did what they could to keep my past alive and to understand and share my culture with me.

Slowly I began talking about that past. Only a month or so after my arrival, I described to Saleen my Indian family in outline – mother, sister, two brothers – and that I'd been separated from my brother and become lost. I didn't have the resources to explain too much, and Saleen gently let me lead where I wanted to go, rather than pressing me. Gradually, as my English improved, I told Mum and Dad a few more things, like the fact that my father had left the family when I was very little. Most of the time, though, I concentrated on the present: going to school, making friends and discovering a love of sport.

Then, one wet weekend just over a year after I'd arrived in Hobart, I surprised Mum – and myself – by opening up about my life in India. Perhaps I now felt safe enough, and had enough English, to talk about my experiences. I told her more than ever before about my Indian family: about how we were so poor that we often went hungry, or how my mother would have me go around to people's houses in the neighbourhood with a pot to beg for any leftover food. It was upsetting, and Mum held me close. She suggested that together we draw a map of the place I was from, and as she drew I pointed out where my family's home was on our street, which way you went to walk to the river where all the kids played, and where the bridge was, under which you walked to get to the train station. We traced the route with our fingers and then drew the layout of my home in detail. We put in where each member of my family slept – even the order in which we lay down at night. We returned to the map and refined it as my English improved. But in the whirl of memories brought on by first making that map, I was soon telling Mum about how I'd become lost. As she looked at me, amazed, she took notes. She drew a wavy line on the map, pointing to Calcutta, and wrote 'a very long journey'.

Perhaps that little hand-drawn map helped me grasp the meaning of the big map of India on my bedroom wall. The hundreds of place names on it swam before me in my childhood. Long before I could read them, I knew that the immense V of the Indian subcontinent was a place teeming with cities and towns, with deserts and mountains, rivers and forests – the Ganges, the Himalayas, tigers, gods! It came to fascinate me. I would stare up at the map, lost in the thought that somewhere among all those names was the place I had come from, the place of my birth. I knew what it was called, or thought I did, but whether the name I knew belonged to a city, or a town, or a village, or maybe even a street, I had no idea. Nor did I have a clue where to start looking for it on that big map.

A couple of months after Mum and I drew our map, we flew to Melbourne to visit some other kids who had been adopted from the same Calcutta orphanage as me. Chattering happily in Hindi to my fellow adoptees brought the past back very vividly. I told Mum I didn't come from Calcutta at all – a train had taken me there from a train station near 'Ginestlay', the name of my home. When she asked me where I was talking about, I confidently, if a little illogically, replied, 'You take me there and I'll show you. I know the way.' I went on to tell her that the train station might have been called something like 'Bramapour', 'Berampur' . . . I wasn't sure. All I knew was that it was a long way from Calcutta and no one had been able to help me find it.

Saying aloud the name of my home for the first time since arriving in Australia was like opening a release valve. Soon after that, I told an even more complete version of events to a teacher I liked at school. Over an hour and a half, she wrote notes too, with that same amazed expression. Strange as I found

Australia, for Mum and my teacher, hearing me talk about India must have been like trying to understand things that had happened on another planet.

I hadn't been aware of how unusual my story was – it was upsetting to me, but I thought it was just part of life. It was only later, when I began to open up to people about my experiences, that I saw in their eyes it was extraordinary.

*

The story I told them was about people and places I'd revisited in my mind again and again since I'd arrived in Australia. As I grew up, I kept thinking about them, keeping the memories fresh. Of course there are gaps – who remembers every detail of their lives in early childhood? Sometimes I'm unsure of details, such as the order in which incidents occurred, or how many days passed between them. But much of my story, and what happened to me when I was a little boy, remains so vivid in my memory that I can see my home, my mother, my baby sister and my two big brothers as if in a bright dream.

2

Hungry and happy

I remember watching over my baby sister, Shekila, her grubby face smiling up at me as we played peekaboo. And I remember long, warm nights outside in the courtyard: my family and the others who shared the house gathering to sing and listen to the harmonium. The women would bring out bedding and blankets, and we would all snuggle together, gazing up at the stars, before closing our eyes to sleep. On those nights I knew I belonged. I was happy.

That was in our first house, where I was born. We shared it with another Hindu family. Each family had part of a large central room, with brick walls and a floor made of mud and straw bound together with cow dung. It was very simple, but it wasn't a slum, and we all got along. Some of my happiest memories are of my time there.

My mother was a Hindu, like most people in India. Hinduism is more than a religion – it's a way of life – and it's one of the oldest in the world. It has many gods, but three main ideas: dharma (being a good person), karma (the good and bad things you do during your life), and reincarnation (being reborn as something either better or worse, depending on your karma). So if you do good (dharma), you'll have good karma and a good rebirth. But if you do bad things, you could come back as a slug.

My father was a Muslim. Muslims believe in one god, Allah, who sent prophets to Earth such as Abraham, Moses, Jesus and lastly Muhammad. Muslims should do five main things: declare their faith, pray, give to charity, fast and go on a pilgrimage to the holy city of Mecca.

At that time, it was unusual for a Hindu and Muslim to marry and the marriage didn't last long. My father spent only a short time with us – I discovered later he had taken a second wife – and so my mother raised us by herself. Although we weren't brought up as Muslims, my mother moved us to the Muslim side of town, where I spent most of my childhood.

My mother was very beautiful, slender, with long, lustrous hair – I remember her as the loveliest woman in the world. As well as my mother and my baby sister, there were also my older brothers, Guddu and Kallu, whom I loved and looked up to.

Our second home was smaller, with the same mud, straw and cow-dung floor, but we had it to ourselves. It was a single room on the ground floor of a red brick building down a narrow, twisting alleyway. It was so badly built my brothers and I could pull out a brick for fun and peer through the hole before sliding it back into place. There was a little fireplace in one corner and a clay water tank in another, for drinking and sometimes washing. We kept our sleeping blankets on the single shelf.

The weather was generally hot and dry, except during the heavy rains of the monsoon, which started in May or June and finished in September or October. A river ran from a range of distant hills past the old town walls, and in the monsoon it would break its banks and flood the surrounding fields. When the river dropped after the monsoon rains ended, we would try to catch little fish in the calmer waters. In town, the monsoon flooded the low railway underpass and it became unusable. At other times, the underpass was a favourite place to play, despite the dust and gravel that sometimes rained down on us when a train passed overhead.

Our neighbourhood was very poor, housing the many railway workers of the town. The streets were broken and unpaved, and some of the buildings were crumbling. There wasn't much that was new. Those who didn't share a communal building lived in one or two rooms like us, furnished in the most basic way with maybe a shelf, a low wooden bed and perhaps a tap over a drain.

Apart from us kids, cows wandered the streets, even in the town centre, where they might sleep in the middle of the busiest roads. Pigs slept in families, huddled together on a street corner at night, and in the day they would be gone, foraging for whatever they could find. It was almost as if they worked nine to five, and clocked off to go home and sleep. You wouldn't know if they belonged to anyone – they were just there. There were goats too, kept by the Muslim families, and chickens pecking in the dust. Unfortunately, there were also lots of dogs; some were friendly, but many were unpredictable or vicious. I was particularly afraid of dogs after one chased me, snarling and barking, down an old pathway. I tripped and hit my head on a broken tile, which sliced open my eyebrow – I was lucky not to lose an eye.

A neighbour patched me up and when I set off for home, I ran into Baba, our local Muslim holy man. He told me never to be afraid of dogs – they would only bite you if they sensed you were scared of them. I tried to be brave, but I was always nervous around dogs after that. My mother had warned me that some dogs had a deadly disease that you could catch from even a small nip. I've still got the scar and I never learned to like dogs.

After my father left, my mother had to work to support us. Soon after Shekila's birth, she went off to work on building sites, carrying heavy rocks and stones on her head in the hot sun, six days a week, from morning until dusk. It meant I didn't see very much of her. Often she had to go to other towns for work and could be away for days at a time. Sometimes we would only see her a couple of times a week. And still she couldn't earn enough money to provide for herself and four children. So when Guddu was about ten, he took a job washing dishes in a restaurant. Even with his earnings, we often went hungry.

Some days we begged for food from neighbours, or begged for money and food on the streets by the marketplace and around the railway station. We survived, living day-to-day and hand-to-mouth. Each morning everyone used to go out and get whatever they could, be it money or food. Each evening we would share what we had found. I remember feeling hungry most of the time, but oddly enough I wasn't too distressed by it. It was part of life and I accepted it. We were very skinny – malnourished like poor children all across India – our empty stomachs swollen with fluids and gas.

My brothers and I were creative about finding things to eat, like a lot of kids in the neighbourhood. Sometimes it was as simple as throwing stones at mangoes, trying to knock one down from someone's tree. At other times we were more adventurous. Walking home one day, we decided to take a back way through the fields and came across a large hen house, with armed guards patrolling it. Guddu thought we could safely grab some eggs, so we made a plan. We would stay hidden until the guards went on a tea break, then I would go into the hen house first, being shorter and harder to spot, and Guddu and Kallu would follow. Guddu told us to use our shirts as baskets and collect as many eggs as we could, then get out and run home.

We watched from our hideout until the guards' break, when they went to sit with the shed workers, eating rotis and drinking chai, a sweet, milky, spiced tea. There was no time to waste. I was first inside and started grabbing eggs. Guddu and Kallu followed. But the chickens started squawking. We dashed out as the guards ran towards the shed. Guddu yelled, 'Run for it!' and we split up and bolted. We were a lot faster than the guards, and luckily they chose not to shoot at us. After sprinting for a few minutes I knew I'd given them the slip and walked the rest of the way home.

Unfortunately, I'd broken all but two of the nine eggs – the rest were dripping down my front. My brothers had beaten me home and my mother had the frying pan on the flame. Between us we had ten eggs left – enough to feed us all. I was ravenous as I watched my mother give the first batch to Shekila. I couldn't help myself – I nabbed a fried egg from my sister's plate and ran out the door, ignoring her ear-splitting cries of protest.

On another occasion, I woke early feeling very hungry and found there was nothing to eat in the house. I remembered seeing a field of ripening tomatoes nearby and set out, determined to have some. It was cool in the early morning air and I still had my sleeping blanket wrapped around me. When I reached the field, I squeezed in through a gap in the barbed-wire fence and within moments I was picking tomatoes, savouring their soft flesh. But then I heard a loud whistle and saw five or six older boys running towards me across the field. I dashed back to the fence, and squeezed through an opening I knew would be too small for them. My prized red blanket snagged on the barbed wire, and with the boys bearing down on me I had no choice but to leave it behind. When I got home my mother was happy I had brought some tomatoes to eat, but furious I had lost my blanket in the process. But she didn't beat me like a lot of parents did; she never raised a hand to any of us.

Another run-in over food almost cost me my life.

I accepted a job ferrying ten large watermelons across the main street for a man with a stall in the town market. He offered me a little money and I hoped he might add a slice of watermelon when I was done. But the watermelons were very large and I was small. Struggling with the first one, I wove through the heavy traffic. *Bang*! I lay on the tarred road, bleeding from the head, with the crimson pulp of the crushed watermelon beside me. It could easily have been my head: I'd gone under the wheel of a speeding motorcycle and injured my leg. The rider took pity on me and gave me a lift home. My mother was horrified when I limped into the house and took me straight to a doctor, who bandaged my wounds.

I don't know how she paid for it.

As they grew up, my brothers spent more time away from Ginestlay, searching for new hunting grounds and sleeping in railway stations and under bridges. Sometimes the holy man, Baba, would look after Shekila and me at the mosque, or he would take me fishing in the river with his long bamboo rod and line. Otherwise, we would be in the care of families who lived nearby, or with Guddu in the restaurant where he scrubbed pots and pans at a tub.

*

Harsh as all this sounds, we were happy enough, although of course we wished things could be different. Often, first thing in the morning, I would go and hang around the gates of the local school, watching the children entering in their uniforms. I would stare through the gate, wishing I could be a pupil, too. But we couldn't afford for me to go to school. I felt shy because I had no education. I couldn't read or write, I spoke poorly and had trouble communicating.

The person I was closest to was my baby sister, Shekila. After a certain age, I had to wash and feed her, and watch over her. Shekila and I used to sleep in the same bed, and when we woke I would fetch her whatever breakfast I could find. We used to play together: peekaboo and hide and seek. Shekila was so tiny and beautiful. She loved being with me and followed me everywhere, and I protected her. Now and then while Guddu worked at various jobs to help earn a little money for the family, Kallu took care of him. The younger brother would ensure that the elder was getting enough to eat and that if he stayed away from home he had a safe place to sleep. With no father around, and our mother often away working, we took care of each other.

For the most part, I stayed within the house and its courtyard. I spent long days sitting on the earthen floor alone, idly listening in on conversations and watching life go on around me, while Shekila slept inside. Sometimes the local townsfolk who kept an eye on us would let me go off and find firewood for cooking, and I would haul it back and stack it by the side of the house. Occasionally I earned a paisa or two – enough for a lollipop – by helping the local storekeeper deliver wooden planks. He'd have me stack them in the pen by the store's front door. But mostly I simply sat alone in that courtyard. We had no TV or radio. There were no books or newspapers, although, of course, I couldn't have read them anyway. It was a simple, basic existence.

Our diet was basic as well: roti bread, rice and dhal, sometimes with a few vegetables tossed in if we were lucky. Fruit grew in our area, but that was a luxury and most of it was sold for cash. There weren't many fruit trees around that we could raid. Like the town's vegetable plots, they were well guarded. We learned to live with hunger, because it was always there.

In the afternoons, kids would come by after school and I was allowed to go off and play with them. Sometimes we'd play cricket on any patch of bare earth we could use.

I also loved to chase butterflies, or fireflies when it got darker. And I loved flying kites – simple things made of sticks and paper – for even a basic kite cost money. So if I wanted a kite, I'd try to spot one stuck in a tree and climb up and get it, no matter how dangerous it was. Then we would stick sand to our kite's string to produce a cutting edge and challenge each other to a kite dogfight. Each of us would try to cut the string of the other's kite as it flew – it was exciting. Kids played marbles too, but again, you needed money to get a marble to start with.

I didn't really have any close friends – perhaps because we had moved, or perhaps because I was not very trusting – so whenever I could, I hung out with my brothers, whom I adored.

As I got a bit older, I was given more leeway outside the house and was allowed to start playing with kids further away. Sometimes I'd leave Shekila at the house for a while, knowing she could safely pass the time by herself while I was out. This is illegal in the West, but in my town it wasn't uncommon when parents had to do other things, and I'd been left like that many times myself so I didn't feel guilty about it.

Like any kid, I stayed close to home at first, so that if anything bad happened I could run home quickly. Eventually, though, I started ranging as far as the town centre. Sometimes my brothers and I would go down to the river below the dam wall, a long walk beyond the edge of town. There we'd watch fishermen netting fish.

By this time, Guddu and Kallu were about fourteen and twelve, and spending very little time at home. I saw them only two or three times a week. Mostly, they were living off their wits, scouring the streets for whatever they could find to subsist on and sleeping in railway stations, where they sometimes earned food or money for sweeping. Usually they stayed at a town a few stops down the train line, about an hour away. They would tell me Ginestlay was no good, and they were going to a place called 'Berampur' (or something like that – I couldn't quite remember its name) where it was easier to find money and food. They had started making friends there, all of them jumping on and off trains whenever they needed to travel.

Railways were the veins of the country when I was

a child, carrying goods, people and money. Trains brought glimpses of the more affluent city life to our backwater town in the middle of rural India. It's not surprising that we spent a lot of time hanging around railway stations watching people come and go. Sometimes we could make a little money by begging or selling things to passengers, as Guddu did with the toothbrush and toothpaste packs that would later get him arrested. The railways were our only connection with the rest of the country, and for most people that's probably still the case.

By the time I was about four or five, my brothers were occasionally taking me along with them. We may not have had much food, but we had a lot of freedom, and we enjoyed it. If a conductor ever asked for a ticket, we'd jump off and then hop on the next train. We'd pass through a couple of very small stations – just platforms in the middle of nowhere – before arriving at Berampur station. It was smaller than Ginestlay's, on the outskirts of town, and my brothers would only let me go as far as the station. I'd hang around the platforms while they worked, then go back home with them. They wouldn't let me go wandering off into town for fear I might get lost. And in India, getting lost can change your life forever.

3

Getting lost

I was five years old the night my life changed. That night, almost the whole family would be gathered for dinner, and although I was tired from a day playing out in the streets, I was excited. My mother was home from work and, more unusually, Guddu had come back to see us. Kallu was the only one missing.

The four of us ate together: my mother, Guddu, Shekila and me. After an hour or so, our mother went out, perhaps to find some more food, and Guddu announced that he was going back to Berampur.

As the eldest, Guddu was the brother I looked up to the most. He'd been away a lot, and I missed him. I missed being part of the gang with my big brothers. The thought of being left behind, as always, a little kid stuck at home with nothing to do, was too much. I jumped up and said, 'I'm coming with you!' I wasn't a little boy anymore, to be left at home while they were out in the world.

It was early evening – if I went with him, there was little likelihood of him getting me back home that night. We'd have to stay together. He thought about it for a moment and then agreed. I was thrilled. We left Shekila sitting on the floor and were gone before my mother returned. She wouldn't worry too much if I was in my brother's care.

Soon, I was laughing as Guddu sped through the quiet streets to the train station, giving me a ride on a bike he'd hired. What could be better? I'd travelled with my brothers before, but that night was different. I was going off with Guddu with no plan to return home and no idea where we might sleep, just like he and Kallu did. I didn't know how long he would let me stay with him, but as we raced through the streets I didn't care.

I still vividly remember the ride. I sat on the bar with my feet braced on either side of the front axle. The road was full of potholes, so it was a bumpy trip, but I didn't mind. There were fireflies in the air, and we passed some kids chasing them. A boy yelled out, 'Hey, Guddu!' but we rode on. I was proud that Guddu was known about town. I had even heard him being mentioned once when I was on a train – I thought he was famous.

We had to watch out for people walking on the street in the dark, especially when we went under the low railway bridge. Then Guddu said we'd walk the rest of the way. Maybe he was tired with me on board. So I hopped off and he pushed the bike along the main street to the station, past the busy chai sellers. When we were near the entrance to the station, Guddu hid the hire bike behind some thick bushes and we walked across the overpass to wait for the next train.

I was already feeling sleepy by the time the train pulled in and we had scuttled aboard. We got as comfortable as we could on the hard wooden seats, but the fun of the adventure was starting to wear off. I rested my head on Guddu's shoulder as the train left the station. It was getting late, and the journey would take an hour or so. I don't know if Guddu was having second thoughts about letting me come, but I was starting to feel a bit guilty, because my mother usually needed me to babysit Shekila while she was at work, and I didn't know when I'd be back.

By the time we got off at Berampur, I was so exhausted I slumped onto a wooden bench on the platform.

'I need a rest. I'm too tired to go on.'

'That's fine,' Guddu said, 'I have to do a few things anyway. Just sit down and don't move. I'll come back in a little while and we can find somewhere to sleep for the night.'

He was probably going to scavenge some food, or hunt for coins around the platforms, I thought. I lay down, shut my eyes and must have fallen asleep straightaway.

When I woke up, it was very quiet and the station was deserted. Bleary-eyed, I looked around for Guddu but couldn't see him anywhere. There was a train at the platform where we'd got off, with its carriage door open, but I didn't know if it was the same one, or how long I'd been asleep.

I was scared to find myself alone at night and still half-asleep. My thoughts were muddled. Guddu wasn't around but he'd said he wasn't going far – maybe he'd got back on the train? I shuffled over and climbed the boarding stairs to have a look. I have a memory of seeing some people asleep on board, and stepping back down in case they woke up and called a conductor. Guddu had said I should stay put, but he was probably on board in a different carriage, working, sweeping underneath the seats. What if I fell asleep on the dark platform again and the train pulled out and I was left alone?

I looked into a different carriage and found no one, but the empty wooden bench seats were more comfortable and felt safer than the quiet station. Guddu would come and get me soon, smiling, perhaps with a treat he'd found while cleaning. There was plenty of room to stretch out. In a few moments, I was sleeping peacefully again.

This time, I must have slept properly. When I awoke, it was broad daylight and the full sun was glaring straight into my eyes. I realised with a jolt that the train was moving – rattling steadily along its tracks.

I jumped up. There was still no one in my carriage, and the landscape outside the barred windows was passing quickly. My brother was nowhere to be seen. No one had disturbed the small boy sleeping alone on a speeding train.

In low-class carriages, you couldn't walk from one carriage to the next, you could only get on and off through the doors at each end. I raced to the end of the carriage and tried the doors on each side – they were both locked. I ran down to the other end – the doors there were locked too.

I can still feel the icy chill of panic that hit me when I realised I was trapped: I was frantic, my heart beating triple-time. I felt weak, wired, anxious and incredulous, all at the same time. I couldn't read any of the signs in the carriage, so I had no idea where I was heading or how to get out. I ran up and down looking beneath all the benches, in case someone else was asleep somewhere, but there was only me. I kept running up and down, yelling my brother's name, begging him to come and get me. I called for my mother, and my brother Kallu too, but all in vain. No one answered and the train didn't stop.

I was trapped.

The enormity of it hit me, and I curled into a ball and cried.

When I stopped crying, I sat in a daze for hours, hurtling along in the empty carriage. Finally I roused myself to look out the window to see if I could recognise some landmarks. The country outside looked similar to the country around my home, but I saw nothing I recognised. I didn't know where I was headed, but I'd travelled much further than ever before. I was already far away from home.

I entered a strange state, perhaps a little like hibernating. I shut down I suppose, exhausted from trying to deal with what was happening. I wept and dozed, and sometimes looked out the window. There was nothing to eat, but there was water to drink from the tap in the filthy toilet cubicles at the rear, with their pit holes open to the tracks below.

Once, I woke up to realise that we'd stopped. At last – I could catch someone's attention on the platform. But there wasn't a soul to be seen. I still couldn't move any of the doors. I beat at them with my fists and screamed and screamed, but the train gave a lurch and started moving again.

Eventually, I was spent – you can't remain in a state of sheer terror indefinitely. I was exhausted, and fell in and out of sleep. It was like a nightmare: awake at the windows, terrified; curled up and drifting in and out of sleep; brief stretches of calm resignation. The train pulled into other stations, but the doors never opened, and somehow no one ever saw me.

But as time passed, perhaps I remembered some of the resilience I'd built up exploring my own town. Perhaps crying helped; perhaps it was my body's way of coping with something my mind and heart couldn't absorb. My body had somehow soothed my feelings, and now, surprisingly, I began to feel a little better. I thought, if I can't get out by myself, then I'll just have to wait until someone lets me out, and then work out how to get home. I would behave like my brothers. They were away for days at a time; I could do that too. They had shown me how to find a place to sleep, and I had looked after myself before, finding things to eat or sell, and begging. Maybe if this train took me away from home, it could take me back home again.

I sat and gazed out the window, trying not to think about anything except the world sliding by outside. I would see where I ended up.

*

Gradually, the countryside became greener than I'd ever seen it before. There were lush fields and tall trees with no branches but great shaggy bunches of fronds at the top. When the sun came out from behind the clouds, everything exploded into bright green light. I saw monkeys running through the tangled undergrowth by the sides of the tracks, and amazing brightly coloured birds. There was water everywhere, in rivers, lakes, ponds and fields. This was a new world to me. Even the people looked different.

After a while, the train began to pass through small towns, and I saw kids playing by the tracks while their mothers cooked or did the laundry on the back step. No one seemed to notice a lone child at the window of the passing train. The towns grew bigger and closer together, and then there was no more open country at all, just more and more houses – streets and streets of them – with roads and cars and rickshaws. There were big buildings too, many more than at home, and buses, trucks, and trains running along other tracks. Everywhere there were people and more people, more than I had ever seen, more than I could ever have imagined living in one place.

Eventually the train slowed, and I knew it must be approaching another station. Was my journey at an end at last?

The train coasted until it was hardly moving at all, then with a sudden lurch it stopped altogether. Wide-eyed, staring from behind the bars of the window, I saw crowds of people swarming on the platform, striding about and hefting luggage. People were rushing everywhere in their hundreds, perhaps thousands, and suddenly, someone opened one of the doors to my carriage. Without a moment's thought, I ran down the aisle as fast as I could and leapt out onto the platform.

At last I was free.

The train had stopped in Calcutta, the sprawling megacity famous for its overpopulation, pollution and crushing poverty, one of the most intimidating and dangerous cities in the world. I'd never heard of the place. I was thrilled to be free of my carriage prison, but frightened out of my wits by the huge station with its pressing crowds.

I was barefoot, in a grimy pair of black shorts and a white, short-sleeved shirt missing several buttons – truly with nothing but the clothes I was wearing. I had no money, no food and no identification of any sort. I was hungry, but I was used to that. What I really hungered for was help.

Frantically, I looked around in the hope of seeing Guddu pushing past all the people to come and rescue me, as if he too might have been stuck on the train for all those long hours. But there were no familiar faces. I had no idea where to go or what to do, except to step out of people's way. I called out, 'Ginestlay? Berampur?' hoping that someone would tell me how to get there. But no one in the seething mass paid me the slightest attention.

At some point, the train I'd arrived on must have pulled away again, but I don't remember noticing. I was paralysed by fear, afraid that if I moved I would only make things worse. I kept to the platform, occasionally calling out, 'Berampur?' But my voice was swallowed up in a confusion of noise, with people shouting and calling to each other, or caught up in lively conversations.

I quickly realised I couldn't understand what anyone was saying. I had grown up in a state where most people speak Hindi; now I was in a city where people spoke mainly Bengali, and almost nobody seemed to speak my language.

Mostly people were just too busy to notice me, pushing on and off trains in the great crush, struggling to get to wherever they needed to go as quickly as possible. One or two people stopped to listen to me, and all I could manage to say to them was something like 'Train, Ginestlay?' Most just shook their heads and walked on. One man replied, 'But "Ginestlay" is where?' I didn't know what he meant – it was just . . . *home*. How could I explain where it was? He frowned and moved on.

A lot of children were begging or hanging around the station looking for whatever they could find, like my brothers back home. I was just one more poor kid, crying something out, too small to make anyone stop and listen.

I steered clear of policemen, out of habit. I was afraid they might lock me up, as they'd once done to Guddu. He'd been arrested for selling toothbrush-and-paste kits at a train station, and the police had put him in jail. He'd been there for three days before we had learned where he was. Conductors, police, anyone in uniform – we'd avoided them all after that. It didn't occur to me that now they might be able to help.

I stayed on the platform even after everyone had left, unable to think what to do next. Nobody had noticed me. I slept on and off, tired and miserable, and sometime during the next day, I gave up trying to find help. It felt as if the people in the station weren't people at all but a great solid mass, like a river or the sky, on which I could make no impact.

I survived by eating scraps of food I found on the ground, like peanuts travellers had dropped or gnawed corncobs that still contained a few kernels, and fortunately it wasn't hard to find taps for a drink. Living in the big station wasn't too different from the way I'd lived before, so although I was often scared and miserable, I knew how to get by, and I suppose my body was used to it.

One thing I knew was that if a train had brought me to where I was, a train could take me back. The way it worked at home was that trains on the track opposite the one you arrived on went back the other way. But I'd noticed that this station was the end of the line, where all the trains came in and stopped, and then chugged back the way they had come. If no one could tell me where the trains went, I would have to find out for myself.

So I boarded the next train that arrived at the platform. Could it be as simple as that? As the train rumbled out, I got a better look at the station: it was a huge red building with many arches and towers, the biggest building I'd ever seen. I was in awe of its size, and hoped I was leaving it and its great crush of people behind forever. But after an hour or so, the train came to the end of its own line, somewhere on the outskirts of the city. Then it switched tracks and went back to the enormous station.

I caught another train and the same thing happened. Maybe the train I needed left from a different platform? There were many more platforms here than at the station near home, and each seemed to have several different kinds of trains – some had lots of compartments with porters helping people on, while others had carriage after carriage filled with people on bench seats, like the one that had brought me here. The number of them was frightening, but one of them must go back to where I'd come from – I just had to find which one.

And so every day – for day after day – I caught a different train out of the city.

To avoid being locked in a carriage again, I travelled only during the day. At the beginning of each trip I would watch the passing scenery hopefully, thinking yes, yes, this feels like the one that will get me home, I've seen that building or those trees before . . . Sometimes the train would reach the end of its journey and then head back again. Other times, it simply stopped at the final station on the line, and I'd be stuck in that unfamiliar, empty place until the next day, when the train began the return journey. I only got off a train if night was falling before it reached the end of the line. Then I'd crawl under the seats inside the station so that I couldn't be easily seen and curl up tight for warmth. Luckily, the weather was never very cold.

I was learning how to live on my own.

And so I shuttled back and forth, trying different platforms, travelling different routes. Sometimes I'd recognise something and realise I'd accidentally caught a train I'd tried before. But all the trips ended in failure.

No one ever asked me for a ticket. Of course, I avoided trains if I saw a conductor on them, just as we did at home, but once I was on, I was never questioned. If an official had stopped me, I might have summoned the courage to ask for help, but none ever did. Once, a porter seemed to understand that I was lost, but when I couldn't immediately make him understand me he waved me off – I wasn't to bother him anymore. The world of adults was closed to me, so I continued to try to solve my problem by myself.

More than anything, I wanted to find my mother, but after a couple of weeks I began to lose heart. My home was out there somewhere, but maybe there was no train from here to there. Or maybe there was some sort of complication I couldn't work out.

All I knew about the city outside the station was what I'd seen from train windows, arriving or leaving. Perhaps there was someone in the city who could help me, give me directions to get home, or even just give me some food. But the masses of people coming and going outside frightened me. Each time I went on a trip to a new and strange place, I was glad to get back to the big station, where I knew my way around and knew where to sleep or where I was most likely to find food. I was adjusting to my new life at the sprawling red station. It felt familiar, and it was the only real connection I had to my home.

I had noticed a group of children who seemed always to be at the end of a particular platform, where they'd huddle together in some old blankets at night. They seemed to be homeless like me, with nowhere else to go, but they didn't try to hide under seats or on trains. I'd watched them, and they had probably seen me, but they had shown no interest in me. I hadn't been confident enough to approach them, but as time passed and I failed to find my way home, I became more desperate. Adults were no use, but maybe other children could help? At least they might let me stay near them, and perhaps I'd be safer with more kids around.

The children weren't welcoming, but they didn't chase me off either, as I lay on a hard wooden seat close to them and rested my head on my hands. Kids on their own were not an uncommon sight here, and one more didn't surprise anyone. I felt more secure with the others nearby and fell asleep quickly.

Before long, though, I was disturbed by what I thought was a bad dream. I heard children screaming, 'Go away, let me go!' Then more shouting – both young and old voices – and in the dim light I thought I could make out a man. He was yelling something like, 'You're coming with me!' Then a child unmistakably screamed, 'RUUUNN!' and I leapt to my feet, knowing this was no dream.

In the confusion, I saw adults grabbing children and carrying them off, and a small girl struggling with a man by the edge of a platform. I ran for my life, sprinting away down a darkened platform and leaping off the end of it, down onto the tracks, before charging into the darkness.

Running almost blind alongside a high wall, I kept glancing over my shoulder to see if I was being chased, but even when I thought there was no one behind me, I didn't slow down. I didn't know what had happened back at the station, or why the men were snatching kids. All I knew was there was no way I was going to be caught.

But there was danger ahead as well as behind. As the track turned to the right, I found myself face-to-face with the blinding lights of a train coming straight towards me.

4

Survival

I jumped to one side as the train hurtled by with a deafening roar, terrifyingly close to my body. I had to press myself as hard as I could against the wall with my face shoved sideways to keep clear of anything that might be sticking out from a carriage. It seemed like an eternity before the last train carriage passed.

I slumped to the ground to catch my breath. Although I was terrified of the dangers in this new city, I'd lived by my wits for long enough not to lose them now. I suppose the advantage of being five was that I didn't think too much about what had happened to the other children, or what it meant, other than that I wanted to avoid it. What choice did I have but to keep going?

I continued to follow the tracks, but more

cautiously. When they crossed a road, I left them – the first time I'd left the rail network since I'd arrived. The road was busy, and I felt safer there than being somewhere out of sight. It soon led to the bank of a huge river over which stretched a massive bridge, dark against the grey sky. It was overwhelming. I'd seen a few bridges from the windows of trains – bigger than the only one I knew from home, which crossed the little river I played in with my brothers – but this was immense.

In the gaps between the shop stalls huddled along the top of the riverbank, I could see the wide expanse of water, busy with boats. The bridge loomed over it, with people streaming along its walkway, and a slow but noisy mass of bicycles, motorbikes, cars and trucks on its road. It was an astonishing sight for a little boy from a small village. How many people were here? Was this the biggest place in the world? I felt more lost than ever now that I'd left the station behind.

I stayed on the street for some time, stunned by the scale of the scene, as the sun slowly rose and the day began. I still seemed invisible to most of the people passing by, but I worried that people like the men I'd just escaped might notice me – or even the very same men, who might be chasing me. Those thoughts gave me the courage to walk past the shop stalls and between some larger buildings, towards the riverbank. The steep grassy slopes, shaded by big leafy trees, quickly gave way to the muddy river's edge, which was full of activity. There were people bathing, or washing pots and bowls in the shallows, or tending small open fires, and porters ferried all manner of things up the banks from long, low boats.

Back home, I had been a very curious child. Once I was old enough to be allowed outside the house on my own, I'd never liked to stay in one place much. I was always keen to see what was around the next corner, which is why I'd been so eager to start living the life of my brothers, on the move and independent, and why I'd quickly chosen to leave the house with Guddu that night. But being lost in the big train station in this huge, alarming city had stifled that curiosity. The city stretched as far as I could see in every direction, and I ached for the familiar streets of home. Now I was afraid to stray too far from the small neighbourhood I already knew. I was torn between going back to the station with its close, confusing streets, and staying in the more open but unfamiliar territory of the riverbank.

Exhausted from the day's frights and lack of proper food and sleep, I kept out of people's way. I had no idea what to do next. I tried hanging around some of the food stalls, to see if anyone might give me something to eat, but they shooed me away.

As the afternoon slipped into evening, I walked along the riverbank a little and came upon a group of people I recognised as holy men sleeping by the river. I'd seen men like these back home. They were not like Baba at his mosque: Baba wore a long white shirt and pants, like many men in my neighbourhood. These men were barefoot and wore saffron robes and beads, and some of them looked quite scary, with wild clumps of long dirty hair wound round their heads and red and white paint on their faces. They were grubby, like me, from living outdoors on the streets. I had been keeping away from adults as best I could, but surely no one bad would find me here, among holy people? I lay down near the men, curled up into a ball, and joined my hands to pillow my head.

Before I knew it, morning had come and I was alone. The holy men had left, but the sun was up and there were people walking about. I had survived my first night on the streets of Calcutta.

*

Hungry as usual, I found that it was easier to find food along the wide river than inside the big red train station where I'd arrived weeks earlier.

The stallholders were indifferent to begging children, so I walked along the water's edge, thinking I might find people cooking there. Not only was it the biggest river I'd ever seen, but it was also fouler and smellier, edged with dead animals, human excrement and filth. I was horrified to see two dead people lying among the piles of rubbish. I'd seen dead bodies before, when people had died at home, but there people treated them respectfully. I had never seen corpses just lying about outside. Here, no one seemed to pay any more attention to dead people than to dead animals.

The sight made me feel sick, but it confirmed what I'd already begun to feel – there was danger everywhere, and in everyone – there were robbers and people who took children and even killers. All sorts of fears began to stir in me. Every day in this city seemed a matter of life and death. Was this the world that my brothers lived in when they went away, and the reason they never let me leave the stations when I travelled with them? What had happened to Guddu at the train station? Where had he got to and why hadn't he been there when I woke up? Was he somewhere like this, looking for me? And what did my family think had happened to me? Were they looking, or did they think I was dead, lost to them forever?

More than anything I wanted to get back to my mother, to Guddu, to our family, to feel safe and cared for once more. But I knew that if I were to have any hope of that I would have to be strong. Otherwise, I might disappear without a trace, or even die, here on the bank of the wide, murky river. I understood then that I could only rely on myself. I had to pull myself together.

I turned back towards the bridge and came to some stone steps leading into the river, where people were bathing and washing their laundry. There was a wide stone drain next to the steps, which brought water and waste down into the river from the street. Kids were playing, splashing and fooling about in the water, so I went over to join in. Many visitors to India wonder how anyone could wash or bathe in a river that is also a sewer and mortuary, but at the time I didn't give it a second thought. It was a river – rivers were for all of those things. They were also sites of extraordinary acts of kindness, as I was to discover.

The other children seemed to accept me joining in and we played about in the water, a relief from the heat of the day. While some were very confident, leaping off the side of the steps out into the river, I only went in up to my knees. My brothers had tried to teach me to swim in the dammed river near our town, but I hadn't managed it yet. Apart from during the monsoon, the river at home was just a gentle stream to splash in. I loved being in the water, and never more than on that day – it felt wonderful to simply be a child again, playing with other kids.

Later in the afternoon, the other children went home. I stayed on the steps, not wanting the day to end. I hadn't noticed, but the water level must have been rising throughout the day, and when I jumped in to what had been shallow water earlier on, I suddenly found myself in much deeper water – over my head. There was a strong current too, which was carrying me further from the steps. Splashing and flailing desperately, I pushed off from the river bottom and struggled back to the surface to gasp a breath of air, but the water dragged me down and away again. This time I was too far out to reach the bottom. I was drowning.

Then I heard a splash nearby and found myself wrenched upwards, pulled to the surface and onto the steps, where I lay spluttering and coughing up murky water. I had been saved by a homeless old man who had jumped in off the stone drain to pluck me from the water, just in time. Then he silently made his way back up the steps and onto the riverbank, where I suppose he lived.

Perhaps the kindness of that stranger lowered my guard, or perhaps I was just a five-year-old, but when I went back to swim in the river the next day, stupidly I let the rising tide and strong current surprise me again, and once more got into trouble. Amazingly, the same man rescued me – perhaps he'd kept an eye out when he saw me come back. This time, other people noticed the man help me up onto the steps, where I hacked up more water. A crowd formed around us, and I understood enough to realise they were declaring that the gods had spared me, that it was not yet my time to die.

I felt overwhelmed by all the people pushing in to stare at me, and humiliated for having almost drowned a second time. I leapt to my feet and ran away as fast as I could, far along the bank, until I couldn't run anymore, vowing to keep out of the river.

I don't think I ever thanked that homeless old man for rescuing me, not once but twice – my guardian angel.

To escape the crowd, I had run away from the area I had come to know, and night was falling. It was too late to try to get back to my part of the riverbank before dark, so I had to quickly find somewhere nearby to sleep. I came upon what looked like a disused factory, with a large pile of rubbish in the shadows at the back. Exhausted, I found a piece of cardboard and lay down on it behind the rubbish heap. The place had a bad smell, but I was becoming used to that by now, and at least I was out of sight.

That night, I was woken by a pack of scary-looking dogs barking under a nearby streetlight. I kept a rock in my hand, and a pile of others within easy reach. I must have fallen asleep like that, because when I woke with the hot sun full in my face, the rocks were still there but the dogs were nowhere to be seen.

*

Over the next little while, I came to know the neighbourhood around the station, including the little shops and stalls where I foraged for food. The smells coming from those shops were irresistible: mangoes and watermelons, fried savouries, and from the sweets stalls gulab jamuns – fried balls of milk and sweet cheese soaked in rosewater syrup – and laddus – sweet fried dough balls. All I could see was people eating: a group of men cracking peanuts and chatting, some others drinking chai and sharing a small bunch of grapes. Hunger gnawed at me then, and I would go to every shopkeeper and beg. They always chased me away, along with the half-dozen or so other children hanging around – there were too many of us to take pity on.

I'd watch people eating – they were poor people like my family, so they didn't usually leave good food behind, but they might drop something or not finish it entirely. There were no bins, so when a person was done with something, they simply threw it on the ground. I worked out what leftovers could be safely eaten, just as back at home my brothers and I knew which food to scavenge on a railway platform. Bits of fried food, like pastry-wrapped meat or vegetable samosa, were pretty safe once you scraped off the dirt, but they were highly prized. The race would be on to snatch up any remains before other scavenging kids. Mostly I relied on things easily spilled, like nuts or spicy bhuja mix, with dried chickpeas and lentils. Sometimes I'd race for a bit of flat bread. Children as desperate as I was struggled over scraps, and sometimes I found myself roughly shoved aside or even punched. We were like wild dogs fighting over a bone.

Although I mostly stayed near the station and the river to sleep, I began to explore a few of the surrounding streets. Perhaps my natural love of wandering was returning, but I also hoped that around every corner there might be something to eat, some source of food that the other street kids hadn't found – a kindly stallholder or a box of rejects from the market.

A place this big was full of possibilities; it was also full of dangers. On one expedition, I found myself in dense blocks of tumbledown houses and shacks cobbled together from bamboo and rusty corrugated iron. The smell was truly awful, as if something had died. I became aware of people looking at me strangely, as if I had no right to be there. A group of older boys were smoking leaf-wrapped cigarettes, and I started to feel unnerved as they stared at me.

One boy, waving his cigarette around, stood up and approached, talking loudly at me. His friends laughed. I couldn't understand a word and stood there, wondering what to do. Then he strode up and slapped my face, twice, as he continued to berate me. Dumbfounded, I started to cry, and he hit me again, hard. I dropped to the ground and cried while the boys laughed.

I realised things could become much worse and that I had to get out of there, so I tried to collect myself. I stood up, turned and started walking away, as you might from a dangerous dog, my face stinging. Maybe if I showed I didn't want to stay they would leave me alone. But when they began to come after me, I broke into a run. Through my tears I made out a narrow gap between two buildings and darted towards it, just as I felt a hurled rock sting my arm.

I wriggled through the gap and emerged into an enclosed yard. There was no way out, and the boys were shouting on the other side. The ground was a sea of garbage, which washed high up the far wall – perhaps high enough for me to climb up it and get out that way. As I picked my way across the yard, the gang appeared through another entrance I hadn't seen. They started picking things out of a rusty bin, and their leader shouted at me. Then the first bottle sailed through the air and smashed against the wall behind me. More bottles followed, exploding around me – it was only a matter of time before someone got their aim right and hit me. Stumbling and ducking, I reached the rubbish heap and mercifully it held my weight. I climbed all the way up, hauled myself onto the wall and ran along it, praying the boys wouldn't follow me. Bottles kept smashing on the wall below and whizzing past my legs.

Maybe seeing me run was sport enough for the gang. They'd chased me off their territory and didn't bother to follow me as I wobbled along as fast as I could. A little further on I found a bamboo ladder leaning against the wall in someone's backyard. I climbed down it and charged through the house and out the front door, past a woman sitting with her baby. She didn't seem to notice me run by, and I headed back towards the bridge as fast as I could.

*

As well as searching for food beside the river, I was always on the lookout for a safe place to rest. Often, when I returned to a place where I'd slept before, there'd be someone already there, so I'd have to move on. At other times, I'd just come across a better spot. I was always tired from sleeping rough and eating very little, and the constant stress of having to be vigilant all the time wore me out.

Picking along the riverbank at twilight one day, I found myself heading under the enormous bridge for the first time. Beneath it, I came across a few small wooden platforms with offerings such as coconut pieces and coins, along with pictures and little statues of a goddess I recognised – Durga, the warrior form of the supreme goddess, Mahadevi. She was seated on a tiger, with her many arms whirling weapons, which in the stories I'd heard she had used to slay a demon. She was a fierce vision to behold, lit by flickering terracotta lamps. But there was also something comforting about the little lights winking in the gathering darkness all around me. I sat there under the bridge, looking out over the river. Ever hungry, I found the offerings too tempting – I collected some of the bits of fruit and coconut and ate them. I also took some coins.

It felt safe near the shrines, and I didn't want to leave. Nearby was a platform of planks hanging over the water. I checked that it was stable, and clambered on. It felt as if I was in a sacred place, where people came to pray to the goddess. Lying on the hard wooden planks, listening to the sound of the river flowing beneath me, I thought about my family and wondered how they were and how they must be wondering about me. But these feelings were different now from when I'd first arrived – less sharp, less painful, but somehow deeper too. Even if home had stayed the same, I was different. I still desperately wanted to get back there, but I wasn't completely swamped by the feeling. Although I hadn't given up hope of returning to my family, I thought more about surviving here and getting through the days. That home – the home I'd lost – felt even further away. Maybe I had come to feel that *this* was my home now, at least for the time being.

When I woke up the next morning, one of the wild-looking holy men in saffron robes was meditating nearby. Soon others arrived and joined him, some stripped to the waist and some carrying long decorated walking sticks. I left quietly. I knew that I had slept in their place and taken some of their offerings, and that maybe they intended the boards over the water to be another little shrine to Durga. But they hadn't harmed me, or even woken me, and in that moment I felt secure in their company, almost as if we were travelling side-by-side on our journeys.

*

Some days, with little else to do, I would go back to the rail yards and wander among the many tracks. There were always others about, looking for whatever they could find or else just filling up their days, like I was. Maybe they were lost too, wondering which track might lead them home. Occasionally, a train would go by, sounding its horn to warn people to get out of its way.

One quiet but very hot day, I walked around until I was dazed from heat, then sat down on a track, almost falling asleep. A man dressed in a grimy white shirt and trousers came over and said something to me. I understood that he was asking me why I was hanging around in such a dangerous place. When I replied in my halting way, he not only understood me, but replied more slowly and carefully, so I could understand him. He said that many children were hit by trains here and killed, and others lost arms and legs. Train stations and railway yards were dangerous places, he said, not playgrounds for children.

I told him that I was lost, and, encouraged by the fact that he seemed to be patient enough to listen and work out what I was saying, I explained that I came from Ginestlay, but no one seemed to know where that was, and now I was alone with no family and no place to live. It was a relief to be able to tell my story to someone for the first time. After listening carefully, he told me he would take me to his home and give me food and water and a place to sleep. I was overjoyed. Somebody had at last stopped to help and was going to save me. I didn't hesitate to go with him.

He was a railway worker and lived in a little shack by the side of the tracks, near the point at which they all converged at the entrance to the immense red station. The shack was made of corrugated iron sheets and panels of thick cardboard nailed to a wooden frame. He shared it with a group of other railway workers, and I was invited to join them all for dinner. For the first time since I had become lost, I sat at a table and ate a warm meal that someone had cooked. It was a lentil dhal with rice, which one of the workers made over a little fire in a corner of the shack. The workers didn't seem to mind that I was there, and didn't complain about having to share their dinner. They were very poor, but they had just enough to allow them to live by different laws from people on the streets. They had a roof, and enough for a plain meal, and a job, however hard it was. They could only offer me a tiny amount, but it made all the difference because of their willingness to feed and house a stranger. It was like crossing into an entirely different world from the one I'd been living in, and all it took to make it was a few sheets of corrugated iron and a handful of lentils. For the second time, it felt like the kindness of a stranger had saved my life.

In the back of the shack was a simple spare bed made out of straw, and I slept there almost as comfortably and happily as if I was already back home. The railway worker had mentioned that he knew someone who might be able to help me, and the next day he said that he had arranged for this man to visit. I was overwhelmed with relief – already it seemed like the last few weeks were a bad dream. Soon I would be home.

I spent the day in the shack after the men headed off to work, waiting for my saviour. As promised, the next day another man turned up, and he also spoke carefully in plain terms I understood. He was well dressed in a neat suit and he laughed when I pointed at his distinctive moustache and said, 'Kapil Dev,' referring to India's cricket captain at the time, whom he looked like. He sat down on my bed and said, 'Come over here and tell me where you are from.' So I did as he asked, and told him what had happened to me. He wanted to know as much as possible about where I was from, so that he could help me find my village, and as I tried my best to explain everything, he lay down on the bed and had me lie down beside him.

My instincts weren't always sound, but they had been sharpened by weeks of living on the streets, making conscious and unconscious decisions about dangers and risks and learning to survive. I trusted my instincts. Perhaps any five-year-old would have begun to feel uneasy, lying beside a strange man on a bed. Nothing bad happened, and the man didn't touch me, but despite the marvellous, intoxicating promises he was making about finding my home, I knew something wasn't right. I also knew that I should pretend to trust him, so I played along. He said that the next day we would go together to a place he knew and he would try to send me back home. I nodded and agreed. At the same time, I knew beyond question that I should have nothing to do with this man, and that I had to make a plan to escape.

That night after dinner, I washed the dishes in a worn old tub in the corner near the door, as I'd done the previous two nights. The men went into their usual huddle for their chai and a smoke, and were soon completely distracted by their conversation and jokes. This was my chance. I picked the best moment I could and bolted out the door. I ran as if my life depended on it, which it probably did. I hoped that if I took them by surprise, I'd get enough of a head start to escape pursuit. Once more, I was fleeing into the night over railway tracks and down streets I did not know, with no idea where to go, and no thought but escape.

I was quickly exhausted and slowed down once I was in crowded streets. Maybe they wouldn't even care that I was gone, and even if they did, surely they couldn't have followed me this far. Then I heard someone call my name from close behind. It sent a jolt through my body like an electric shock. I ducked down, although I was already much shorter than the people all around me, and headed for the most crowded parts of the narrow street, near the bustling stalls hawking food along the curb. When I looked around, I glimpsed a couple of men who looked like they might be following me – grim, hard-faced men, glancing around and moving fast. I realised one of them was the railway worker I'd met first, who no longer looked like the kind man who'd taken me in. I hurried away from them, but the street soon became so crowded it was hard to move quickly, and I felt that the men were getting closer. I had to hide. I found a small gap between two houses and ducked into it, crawling back as far as I could, before I came to a leaking sewerage pipe in one of the walls large enough for me to hide in. I backed into it on all fours until I couldn't be seen from the street, ignoring the cobwebs and the foul-smelling water running over my hands. I was much more scared of what was out there than I was of the dark pipe.

If they found me there was no way out.

5

Very lucky

I heard one of the men talking to the fruit-juice seller whose stand was right next to where I was hidden. I peered out just as the railway worker himself glanced towards the pipe, searching with hard eyes that seemed for a moment to stop on me, and after a moment's hesitation, moved on. I had trusted that man and believed that he was going to help me, only for the ground to open and try to swallow me up. I would never forget that terrifying feeling.

I stayed hidden for some time, until I was certain he and the others had left, then slipped out and made my way through the darkest of the alleys and streets. I was extremely relieved to have escaped, but heartbroken that all my hopes had come to nothing. My survival instincts were strong, and at some level, I took strength from being able to look after myself.

*

I was so scared of being found by the railway worker and the other men that I didn't dare stay anywhere near the railway station. Until then I had been too cautious to move far from the point at which I had first arrived in the city, despite my occasional forays into the nearby neighbourhood. But now I had to. I decided to cross the river for the first time.

The walkways on either side of the long bridge were as crowded as the station platforms, but with many different types of people. Most were hurrying to and fro, by themselves or in groups, looking very busy, but some were just hanging around as though they lived there, high above the water.

I had to dodge families shuffling along in knots and people ferrying enormous piles of goods on their heads. I passed beggars missing limbs and eyes, some with faces ravaged and eaten away by disease, all with their metal begging bowls calling up for a rupee or some food. The road in the middle was crawling with traffic of all kinds, including rickshaws and bullock carts, and even stray cows wandered through the fray.

The scale of it all overwhelmed me. I pushed through as best I could, and got off the main road as soon as I was on the other side.

Now in quieter surroundings, I wandered a maze of alleys and streets aimlessly, keeping watch for both trouble and help. The railway worker had made it harder for me to tell the difference. Although I now had some faith in my street smarts, the experience with the railway man had taught me that I couldn't survive on my own for very much longer – the dangers were too great and too hard to see. My suspicions about people had been reinforced – they were either indifferent or bad – but so had my need to find that rare person who could genuinely help me, like the homeless man by the river. I wanted to stay away from people but also find help. That meant I needed to stay extremely alert. The combination of wariness and the need to take a chance would characterise the rest of my journey.

I began to approach people a little more. Once, walking along one of the streets of my new neighbourhood, I came across a boy about the same age as me, talking aloud to himself, or to the world at large. When he saw me watching him, he said hello and we talked shyly for a bit. He seemed to know more words than I did, to speak more like an adult, so he probably went to school, but he was friendly and we played around on the street for a while. Then he said I could go with him to his house. Cautiously, I followed.

When we got there, he introduced me to his mother, and I told them a little of what had happened to me. The mother told me that I could share a meal with them, and maybe stay with them until they could find someone who might be able to get me home. My wariness slipped away in the face of what seemed genuine concern. I couldn't imagine the friendly woman meaning me any harm, and here was a chance to get off the streets. Even that short time in the railway worker's house had broken the habits of sleeping rough – now I wanted the safety of being inside even more. I felt very happy that I was in a home, fed and sheltered.

The next day the mother said I could go out with her and her son, and we walked to a pond nearby, where the locals did their laundry. She set about washing their clothes, and the boy and I washed ourselves too. I had worn the same black shorts and short-sleeved white shirt since I'd become lost, and I must have been very dirty. I loved being in water where I didn't need to be able to swim, and as usual I could have stayed there forever. But the day wore on, and my new friend got out and was dried and dressed when his mother started to call for me to join them. Perhaps I'd forgotten the ways of families and the respect owed to a mother's authority, but I kept splashing about, not wanting to leave. The mother quickly lost her temper and flung a rock that missed me by a whisker. I started to cry, but the mother took her son, turned and left.

Standing there in the shallows of the pond I wondered if I had misunderstood something. Maybe by staying in the water I had made them think I didn't want to join them. My mother would never have thrown a rock at me, even if she thought I was misbehaving. But the woman had turned her back on me with the same ease with which she had welcomed me into her house. Was this just how people were in the big city?

Although they had left me on my own again, meeting them had still been good: as well as being given another proper meal and a place indoors to sleep, I had discovered that there were perhaps more people than I'd first thought who could be made to understand what I was saying. And, not long afterwards, I found another.

One day I was hanging around near a shopfront in my new neighbourhood in the hope of scavenging some food, when a boy about the age of my brother

Guddu came along, wheeling a handcart piled with goods. I have no idea what made him notice me, but he said something to me I didn't understand. He wasn't aggressive at all, so I didn't panic; I just stood and looked at him as he walked over. Then he spoke more deliberately, asking me my name and what I was doing.

We talked for a bit and I admitted I was lost, and he invited me to stay with his family. I might have hesitated, wondering whether he meant me harm or would turn on me, as the little boy's mother had, but I went with him. It was a risk, but so was staying on the streets. And my instincts told me this boy meant well.

I was right. He was very friendly, and I stayed at his family home for several days. Sometimes I went out with him and helped with his work lugging goods on and off his cart, and he was patient and seemed to be looking out for me. I soon learned that he was doing much more for me than that.

One day he began talking with me in what seemed like a different way – more adult, more serious. He told me he was taking me to a place where I might be able to get help, and we went across town together. When I saw that he'd brought me to a large police station, I immediately began to resist. Was this a trick? Was he having me arrested? The teenager calmed me down, promising that the policemen didn't mean any harm, that they would try to find my home and family. I didn't really understand what was going on, but I went inside with him. The teenager spoke to the police for some time, and eventually came back to me to say that he was going to leave me in their care. I didn't want him to go – I was still very nervous about the police – but my trust in this boy was strong enough to allow me to stay. I didn't know what else I could do. I was sad and scared when he said goodbye, but he said he'd done all he could, and that this was the best way for me to find my way home.

Soon after the teenager left, I was taken out the back of the station to the lockup, where I was locked in a cell. I had no idea if things were taking a turn for the better or worse. I didn't know it then, but the teenager had saved my life, just as the homeless man by the river had done.

Sometimes I wonder what would have happened to me had he not taken me in, or had I refused to trust him. It's possible someone else would have done the same thing he did, eventually, or that I would have been collected by some organisation for homeless kids. But it's more likely I would have died on the street. Today, there are perhaps a hundred thousand homeless kids in Kolkata (the Bengali name for

Calcutta), and a good many of them die before they reach adulthood.

Despite the many memories that I wish I could forget, I have always wished I could remember one thing: that teenager's name.

*

I slept that night in the police lockup. The next morning, some policemen came and reassured me that I wasn't under arrest or in trouble, and that they were going to try to help. I felt uneasy, but I went along with what they said. It was to be my first step on a journey that would take me halfway around the world.

I was given food, then put into a big paddy wagon with other children, both older and younger than me. We were driven through town to a building where some official-looking people gave us lunch and a drink. They asked me lots of questions, and although I didn't always understand them, it was clear that they wanted to know who I was and where I had come from. I told them what I could. They recorded my answers on many forms and documents. 'Ginestlay' meant nothing to them. I struggled to remember the name of the place where I'd boarded the train but could only say my brothers called it something like 'Burampour', 'Birampur', 'Berampur' . . .

Although they took notes, they didn't really have a hope of finding these half-remembered names of comparatively tiny places that could be anywhere in the country. I didn't even know my full name. I was just 'Saroo'. In the end, without knowing who I was or where I'd come from, they declared me 'Lost'.

After they finished their questioning, I was taken in another van to another building, a home that they said was for children like me, who had nowhere else to go. We pulled up outside a massive rusted iron door, like a prison gate, with a tiny doorway in the wall next to it. I wondered whether, if I went in there, I would ever come out. But I'd come this far; I didn't want to go back to the streets.

Inside, there was a compound of large buildings called 'the home'. The building I was taken to was immense – two storeys with hundreds, maybe thousands, of children playing or sitting in groups. I was taken into a huge hall with rows and rows of bunk beds stretching its length. Way down the end of the hall, there was a communal bathroom.

I was shown to a bunk bed with a mosquito net, which I would be sharing with a little girl, and given food and drink. At first the home seemed just how I had imagined school to be, but this school had rooms with beds, and you lived there – a little more like a hospital, or even a prison. Over time it would come to feel more like a prison than a school, but at first I was happy to be there, and to be sheltered and fed.

I soon learned that there was a second hall above mine with just as many bunks, also filled with kids. Often we slept three or four to a bed, and were sometimes moved around so we ended up sharing with different kids, or sleeping on the floor if there were too many kids in the home. The bathrooms weren't cleaned often. The whole place was eerie, especially at night, when it was all too easy to imagine ghosts hiding in every corner.

I wonder now whether the feel of the place was somehow connected with what so many of the children had been through. Some had been abandoned by their families, and others had been taken away from families who had hurt them. I started to feel like I was one of the luckier ones. I was malnourished but not sickly, whereas I saw children with no legs or no arms, and some with no limbs at all. There were others with awful injuries and some who could not, or would not, speak. I'd seen people with deformities before, and mentally ill people yelling out to no one or acting crazily, especially on the streets around the station. But I could always avoid them if I was scared. In the home, I couldn't get away – I was living with kids with all manner of problems, including criminal and violent children who were too young to be jailed. Even so, some were almost adults.

I later learned that this was a juvenile detention centre, called Liluah, housing problem children of any and all kinds, including those who were lost, but also the mentally ill, thieves, murderers and gang members. But back then I just knew it as a distressing place, where I would wake in the night to someone screaming, or lots of frightened kids crying. What would become of me here? How long was I going to live in this horrible place?

Again, I had to learn how to survive. Just as I had been picked on by boys outside, I was picked on by older boys in the home from the outset. Not having much of a vocabulary made me vulnerable, and my smallness and relative defencelessness brought out the bully and the brute in them. Bigger boys would start taunting and making fun of me, and then push me, and if I didn't manage to get away, I would be bashed. I quickly learned to stay away from certain areas at playtime. The staff didn't seem willing to intervene, but when they did, punishment would be meted out without regard for who was to blame: a long, thin cane was fetched, which hurt doubly, because the split end pinched your skin with every blow.

There were other dangers, too, which I avoided more by luck than by planning.

I know now that few children are saved from the streets, and many of those who are rescued still have a lot of suffering ahead of them.

In the few weeks I was at the Liluah home, some kids left through the little door in the wall, but I was never really sure why they were allowed to leave or where they would be going. Maybe someone had found their families? I wondered what happened to the older ones who grew into adults within the walls. Perhaps they were sent to a different place, or just released onto the streets once they reached a certain age.

I prayed that, for whatever reason, I would be one of those who got to leave before I grew up.

And eventually I was. About a month after I arrived, the authorities decided to hand me over to an orphanage. No one had reported me missing and they didn't know where I was from – I was a mystery. All I knew was that I was called into the main office and told I was going to another home, a much nicer one. I was sent off to shower and was provided with new clothes. As always, I did as I was told. They said

I was very lucky. And, although they didn't seem to have found my family, I did indeed feel very lucky to be leaving what I'd come to think of as a hellish place.

*

The woman who fetched me was called Mrs Sood, and she took me to an orphanage called Nava Jeevan, which is Hindi for 'new life'. She was from ISSA – the Indian Society for Sponsorship and Adoption – and she was to become a major figure in my life. She explained that the authorities had no idea who I was or where my home and family were, but she was going to try to find them, in places that might be the 'Berampur' I had told them about.

Nava Jeevan did turn out to be much nicer than the Liluah juvenile home, and was populated mostly by little children like me. It was a blue three-storey concrete building that from the start was far more welcoming. As we walked in, I saw a few other kids inside peering around a corner to see the new arrival – they smiled then ran off when the woman who greeted Mrs Sood and me shooed them away. I could see into a few rooms as we walked by, where the sun streamed in on the bunk beds – far fewer than those in the long halls at the home. The windows had bars, but I was beginning to understand that these were for keeping us safe rather than imprisoned. Colourful posters on the walls also made it seem a much friendlier place.

Although there were fewer children living here than in the home, it was still sometimes overcrowded at night, and some kids were forced to sleep on the floor. This meant you might wake up damp from some other child's pee. In the mornings, we had a quick wash with water pumped from a well near the building's entrance and brushed our teeth using our fingers as a toothbrush. We were given a glass of hot milk with sweet Indian bread or a few milk biscuits. To know that each morning I would start the day with a small meal made me very happy.

It was usually quiet during the day, when many of the others went off to school. Because I had never been to school, I was left behind, sometimes alone. I spent a lot of time hanging around on the front porch, which was enclosed with bars like a cage. I liked the view of a large pond across the street. After a while, I got to know a girl about Guddu's age who lived on the other side of the pond, and she sometimes came to visit. Occasionally, she'd pass me a snack between the bars, and one day she gave me a necklace with a pendant of the elephant-headed god, Ganesh. I was astonished. It was the first present I'd ever received from anyone. I kept the necklace hidden from the others, occasionally taking it out to gaze at in wonder. I later learnt that Ganesh is often called the Remover of Obstacles, and Lord of Beginnings. I wonder whether that was why the girl chose to give it to me. (Ganesh is also Patron of Letters, and so, in a way, he is the patron of this book.)

The necklace was more than just a beautiful object to call my own; for me, it proved that there were good people in the world who were trying to help me. I still have it and it's one of my most treasured possessions.

There were bullies at the orphanage, of course, just as there had been at the home, although they were closer to my own age and I was able to keep clear of them. I generally stayed out of trouble, but one time a girl decided to run away and took me with her. I'd never thought to try to get away, but she swept me up in her plan, and we fled out through the doors together one morning before I knew what was happening. We got as far as a sweets stall a little way down the street, where the vendor gave us each a treat to slow us down while he alerted the Nava Jeevan staff to our whereabouts. I don't remember being punished in any way. In fact, no one was ever smacked at the orphanage, let alone caned, though you might get a dressing-down or be made to sit alone for a spell if you misbehaved.

*

It wasn't long before Mrs Sood told me that, despite their efforts, they hadn't managed to find my home or my family and there was nothing more they could do. Mrs Sood seemed very friendly, and I believed she was trying to help, but she said they hadn't found my mother or Berampur. She said they were going to try to find another family for me to live with. As I struggled to make sense of what she was saying, I began to see the hard truth: she was telling me I would never go home.

*

I wondered why these adults couldn't just find the right train to take me back to where I'd come from. I was sad at Mrs Sood's news, but I don't remember being devastated by it, despite its finality. Part of me had already accepted that my family was lost to me. My initial desperation to get home had long faded, and with it the feeling that, unless the world was immediately put back the way it had been, I couldn't exist. My world was now what I saw around me, the situation I was in. Perhaps I had learned some of the lessons my brothers had learned when they started living on their wits away from home. I was younger and didn't have the safety net our mother provided, but we all spent our days struggling to stay alive. I'd concentrated on what I needed to do to survive, keeping my eye fixed on what was in front of me, not far away.

Mrs Sood told me that families from other countries were happy to have lost Indian children live with them, and she thought she could find a new family for me, if I wanted that. I didn't give it too much thought – I'm not sure I really understood what she was telling me.

Four weeks after I'd first come to Nava Jeevan, I was taken to the ISSA office, where Mrs Sood told me she'd found a mother and father who wanted to take me into their home. They lived in another country – Australia. She said that it was a country India played at cricket, which I'd heard before, but I knew no more about Australia than that. Mrs Sood said that two boys I knew who had recently left – Abdul and Musa – had gone there, and that a friend I had made – Asra – had also been chosen to go there. Australia was a good place that was helping poor children without families and giving them opportunities most children in India would never have.

Back at Nava Jeevan, Asra and I were each shown bewitching little red photograph albums made by the people offering to become our new families. Inside were pictures of them, their houses and other aspects of their lives – I looked through mine with my eyes popping out of my head. The people looked so different from what I was used to – they were white! And everything around them looked shiny, clean and new. Some of the things I'd never seen before, and the staff explained to Asra and me what they were, reading us the English captions. In my book it said: 'This is your father washing our car, in which we will visit many places.' They had a car! 'This is the house that will be our home.' It was very grand, with lots of glass windows, and it looked brand new. The book was even addressed to me: 'Dear Saroo.' The family, I was told, were called Mr and Mrs Brierley.

There was also a picture of a jet plane ('This plane will bring you to Australia'), which fascinated me. Back at home, I had seen jets flying high in the sky, leaving their vapour trails streaking behind them, and had always wondered what it would be like to sit in a plane up in the clouds. If I agreed to go to these people, I would find out.

It was overwhelming. Asra was very excited and often asked to see our books, which were held by the staff for safekeeping. She would sit down with me and open hers, point to a picture and say, 'This is my new mum' or 'This is my new house'. I would join in: 'This is *my* new house! This is *my* new dad's car!' We encouraged each other, and her enthusiasm rubbed off on me. It was a little like having a storybook all about me, even though I wasn't in it. It was hard to believe it was real. All I knew about Australia was in that red book, but I really couldn't think of anything else to ask.

At Nava Jeevan, everyone cried from time to time about the parents they had lost. Some children's parents had abandoned them, and some had died. I just didn't know where my family was, and no one could help me find them. It seemed we had all lost our families and there was no going back. Now I was being offered a chance to join a new family. Asra was already talking about hers with enthusiasm.

I don't know that I was truly given a choice, and I'm sure some gentle persuasion would have been brought to bear had I expressed doubts. But it wasn't necessary. I knew there wasn't much I could do if I didn't accept this opportunity. Go back to the home where I was bullied? Go back to the streets and keep taking my chances? Keep searching for a train not even the adults could find?

I told them I wanted to go.

*

My agreeing to join the new family made everyone so happy that the mood was infectious: immediately, any last doubts I had melted away. I was told that I'd be going to Australia very soon, to meet my new parents, and on a jet plane just like the one in the picture.

Asra and I were about the same age, but the others going to Australia were only toddlers or babies. I don't know if that made what was happening more or less scary for the littler ones – how much did they understand?

One day, we were washed and dressed nicely, and some of the boys and girls were taken in separate taxis. The boys went to the house of a woman we were told to call Aunty Ula. She was a white woman from Sweden, although of course that meant nothing to me, but she welcomed us in Hindi, the official language of India, spoken across most of northern and central India. Her house was better than anything I'd ever seen, with rich-looking furniture, curtains and carpet – something like the photos in my red book.

We sat at a dining table and I was presented for the first time with a knife and fork and taught how to use them correctly – I'd only ever eaten with my hands before. We also learned some table manners, such as sitting up straight, not getting up in the middle of a meal, or leaning over to reach for things. After the visit to Aunty Ula's we were even more excited about the adventure we were about to embark upon.

We didn't receive any lessons in English, although at Nava Jeevan there was a pictorial alphabet wall chart, with 'A is for Apple' and so on. I think I was taught to say 'Hello', but there was no time for more than that – I was due to leave India almost immediately. I was going to a place I had been told was far away, at the other end of the world. No one ever talked about my coming back, and no one seemed to be concerned.

Everyone agreed I was very lucky.

6

A new life

So I left India only a few days after I was told of my adoption and a couple of months after I had arrived at the orphanage. There were none of the regulations and delays that are part of inter-country adoptions now. Six of us were flying to Australia from Nava Jeevan, including my friend Asra, and two more children from a different orphanage joined us. Our journey was from Calcutta (now Kolkata) to Bombay (not yet known as Mumbai), then Singapore and on to Melbourne, where our new families would meet us. Asra's new family lived in Victoria, and my new family, the Brierleys, were a second trip away, in Tasmania.

I was sad to say goodbye to Mrs Sood. Three Australian volunteers and someone from an

Australian government department would escort us on the flight. They were all very friendly, and although we couldn't communicate easily, we were so excited about the journey we didn't have time to worry.

I was over the moon when I finally boarded that huge plane. It seemed impossible that such an enormous thing with so many seats and so many people could fly. We were each given a chocolate bar, an amazing luxury for me, which I carefully eked out over the entire trip. We talked and watched a film with headphones on. I was fascinated by the plug in the armrest and being able to control the channel and the volume. We ate everything we were given under those little foil lids – the fact that people brought food to us meant our new life had already begun. I guess we slept.

In Bombay, we stayed overnight in a hotel. It was probably a regular hotel, but to me it was amazing – the most luxurious place I'd ever seen. The room smelled so fresh, and I had never slept in such a soft, clean bed in my life. Despite the excitement and upheaval, I had the best sleep I'd had for months. I marvelled at the bathroom, with its shiny shower and toilet. Around the hotel I saw more white people than I'd ever seen in one place, and they all looked rich to me.

The next day, I was given a new pair of white

shorts and a 'Tasmania' T-shirt, which had been sent by my new parents, to wear on the plane to Australia. I was delighted with my outfit. Better still, we were taken to a toyshop nearby, where we were invited to choose a toy each. I still have the little car I chose, with the pullback mechanism that launched it across the room.

Far below, as we had flown from Calcutta to Bombay, was my home town. The plane I was on must have left one of those vapour trails I had watched with such fascination. I wonder if my mother unknowingly looked up just then and saw my plane and its shining white tail. She would have been astonished beyond belief to know I was on board, and my destination.

*

We landed in Melbourne on the night of 28 September 1987. Our escorts told us our new families were waiting to meet us in a VIP area, and led us through the vast airport.

I felt very shy as I walked into that room. Lots of adults were watching us, but I immediately recognised the Brierleys from the photos I had pored over in my red book. I tried to smile as I stood there, then looked down at the last bit of my precious chocolate bar in my hand.

An escort took me across the room to my new parents. And the first word I said to them? 'Cadbury'. In India, Cadbury is synonymous with chocolate. After we hugged, Mum got straight to work being a mother and produced a tissue to clean my hand.

At Nava Javeen I spoke basic Hindi, and most people in Calcutta spoke Bengali. Because I didn't really speak English when I arrived, and my new mum and dad didn't speak any Hindi, we couldn't talk to each other. So instead we sat together and looked through the red book they'd sent me. Mum and Dad pointed out the house I would live in and the car we would travel in, and we began to get used to each other. Photographs of me on that day show a solemn child who must have been difficult to reach – cautious and reserved after everything I'd been through. I was not alarmed or anxious, especially, just a bit withdrawn, waiting to see what would happen. But despite all this, I knew immediately I was safe with the Brierleys. It was just intuition – they had a quiet, kind manner and there was a warmth in their smiles that put me at ease.

Seeing Asra sitting happily with her family also calmed me. When she left the airport with them, we said goodbye in the cursory way children do.

I spent my first night with my new family sharing a room in the airport hotel, because our short flight from Melbourne over Bass Strait to Hobart was booked for the following day. Mum put me straight in the bath, lathering me up and dousing me in lotions to kill nits and the like. Physically, I was in poorer condition than Australian kids. In addition to the external parasites, it turned out I had an intestinal tapeworm, broken teeth and a heart murmur, which happily didn't last. Being poor in India takes its toll on your health, and living on the streets wears you out even more.

I slept soundly that first night in Australia – clearly I was getting used to hotels. When I opened my eyes next morning, Mum and Dad were watching me from their bed, waiting for me to stir. At first, I just peered out at them from under the sheets. Afterwards, when I was still small and we'd recall that first night as a family, I'd remind them, 'I peeping, I peeping.' Mum would describe how she and Dad raised their heads from their double bed to watch the little mound of sheets with the mop of black hair sticking out, and how every now and then I would peep out at them.

Perhaps none of us could quite believe it was happening – that these strangers in the room were going to be my parents, or that this boy from India was going to be their son.

*

After breakfast, it was back on a plane for the short flight to Hobart, where I got a first look at my new country outside a hotel or airport. To eyes used to the crush and pollution of one of the most overpopulated places on earth, it seemed so empty and so *clean* – the streets, the buildings, even the cars. There wasn't a soul to be seen as dark-coloured as me, but then there was hardly anyone to see at all. The place looked almost deserted.

As we drove through the unfamiliar countryside and into Hobart's suburbs, I saw a city of gleaming palaces, and one of those palaces was my new home. I recognised it from the red book, but it looked even bigger and more impressive in reality. Inside there were four bedrooms for only three people, each of the rooms huge and neat and clean. A carpeted living room, with comfortable couches and the biggest TV I'd ever seen, a bathroom with a big bath, a kitchen with shelves full of food. And a refrigerator: I loved standing in front of it just to feel the cold air come out whenever it was opened.

Adapting to a Western lifestyle seemed easy most of the time, with Mum and Dad's guidance, and they say I settled in well. At first we ate a lot of Indian food, and Mum slowly introduced me to an Australian diet. But there were some big differences between Australian and Indian customs and beliefs: when I noticed Mum putting red meat into the refrigerator once I ran up to her crying, 'Cow, cow!' For a child brought up a Hindu, to slaughter the holy animal was taboo. For a moment she didn't know what to do, but then she smiled and said, 'No, no, it's beef.' Apparently this trick set my mind at rest. In the end, the delight I took in having abundant food close at hand overcame most matters of taste or culture.

One of the best aspects of life in Australia was spending time in the bush or at the beach. In India, I was always in a town or city – often free to roam but nevertheless surrounded by buildings and roads and people. In Hobart, my parents were very active, taking me to play golf or to go birdwatching or sailing. Dad often took me out on his small catamaran, which only increased my love of the water, and I finally learned to swim. Just being able to look out at the horizon gave me peace of mind. India was so choked, you often couldn't see anything but the press of buildings around you – it was like being in a giant maze. For some the bustle of busy cities might be exciting, but you see a different side of them if you're begging or trying to make people stop and listen to you. So, once I got used to it, I found the space in Hobart reassuring.

We lived in the suburb of Tranmere, across the river from central Hobart, and after about a month I started school in the next suburb, Howrah. Only years later did I realise the incredible coincidence. A couple of months before I arrived in Australia, I'd been surviving on the streets of Calcutta in an area also called Howrah, which gives its name to the city's huge red railway station and famous bridge. The Hobart Howrah is a pretty beachside suburb, with schools, sport clubs and a large shopping centre. Apparently an English army officer who had served in Calcutta named it in the 1830s when he came to live in Hobart and saw something in the look of the hills and the river that reminded him of India. If there was any resemblance then, it's lost now.

*

I loved school. There's no free education in India – I probably never would have made it to school without coming to the Tasmanian Howrah. Like the rest of the community, it was quite an Anglo-Saxon place, although there were a couple of kids from other countries. I had extra English lessons along with a student from China and one from India.

I became used to the change of colour and culture around me, but for everyone else, I stood out, especially with my white parents. Other kids talked about their families and how they came from the country, or from Melbourne. When they asked me where I was from, all I could say was 'I'm from India.' But kids are curious – they wanted to know why I was here with a white family. Mum defused a lot of this by attending a parent and student day and telling them about my adoption. It seemed to satisfy my classmates and they didn't ask much after that.

I don't remember any racism at school. Mum, however, tells me there was some that I didn't understand properly. Perhaps there were advantages to not knowing the local language at first. One time, as we were lining up to register me for a sports team, Dad heard the woman in front of him say, 'I don't want him in the same team as that black boy.' I don't mean to make light of comments like that, but compared with what I've heard about other people's experiences, I don't think I had it too bad, and I grew up without any scars from racism, as far as I could tell.

That might not have been true for Mum and Dad. There was quite a large Indian community in Hobart, from Fiji and South Africa as well as India itself, and for a time we went along to the local Indian Cultural Society, which conducted dinners and dances and other events. My parents noticed that we were treated a little suspiciously, and guessed that these people considered it somehow wrong for an Indian child to be taken from India by white parents. Needless to say, I was oblivious to all this.

Another organisation we were involved in was ASIAC, the Australian Society for Intercountry Aid (Children), which helped people adopt from overseas. Mum helped other Australian families with the constantly changing requirements, as well as the personal challenges. Through that organisation, I met other children who'd come to Australia from elsewhere and now lived in mixed-race families. At our first ASIAC picnic I was surprised – and perhaps a little put out – to discover I wasn't the only 'special one' in Hobart. Despite that humbling life lesson, I made friends, one of whom was Ravi, another Indian boy, who lived with his new family in Launceston; our families visited each other often during those early years.

ASIAC also put me back in touch with some of the other kids from Nava Jeevan. My closest friend, Asra, had ended up with a family in the riverside Victorian town of Winchelsea, and we kept in touch by phone.

A year after I arrived, all of us met up in Melbourne with two of the other kids who had been adopted into Australia, Abdul and Musa, for a trip to the zoo. I was overjoyed to see familiar faces, and we all busily compared notes on our new lives, measuring them against our time in the orphanage. Although it hadn't been a terrible place, I don't think any of us wished ourselves back there. It seemed to me that each of them was as happy as I was.

Later the same year, Mrs Sood herself arrived in Hobart, escorting another new adoptee, Asha, whom I remembered from the orphanage. I was so happy to see Mrs Sood again – she'd taken good care of us, and until I left India she was probably the most friendly and trustworthy person I'd met since I'd become lost. I'm sure she enjoyed seeing some of the children she'd helped living in their new homes. Mrs Sood had to deal with a huge amount of trauma among her charges, but the rewards must have been equally large.

*

The person I missed most from India was my sister. When I was asked what I wanted for Christmas, I would sometimes say, 'I want Shekila back.' Of course, I missed my mother deeply, but, from the first, Mum had done a brilliant job of being a mother to me, and having a father's attention made me very happy. They couldn't replace my birth mother, but they did lessen the loss as much as they could. The one person really absent from my life, was a brother or sister. In India my father was absent, and I'd been left for long periods without my mother, but I'd rarely been without my little sister. Shekila had been my special responsibility. She was the member of the family I was most closely bonded with, and was most haunted by. I would sometimes say how guilty I felt for not looking after her as well as I might have done. Perhaps I had in mind the night I left with Guddu.

I was keen on the idea of having a sibling, and when I was ten, Mum and Dad adopted a second child from India. In their application to adopt me, they were happy to have whatever child needed a home – boy, girl, toddler, child, it didn't matter – and that's how they got me. So they did exactly the same thing the second time. We might have been sent a young girl, or an older child, but as it happened, we got my little brother, Mantosh.

I didn't care that he wasn't a sister – the idea of having another child to play with at home was enough for me. And – assuming he'd be rather quiet and shy like me – I thought I could help him adjust to this new life. He'd be someone for me to help look after.

But although Mantosh and I were close in age – only a year apart – we were very different, partly because of the natural differences between people, but also because of our different experiences in India. I was reticent and reserved; Mantosh, at least at first, was loud and disobedient. I wanted to please; he rebelled.

What we did share was the mystery of our past: much of Mantosh's background was unknown, like much of mine. He'd also grown up poor and with no formal education, and can't say for sure exactly where or when he was born. He arrived as a nine-year-old with no birth certificate, medical records or any official documentation of his origins. We celebrate his birthday on 30 November, because that's the day he landed in Australia. Like me, it was as if he simply fell to earth, but, luckily for him, he landed in the care of the Brierleys in Hobart.

The story we now know is this: Mantosh was born somewhere in or near Calcutta and grew up speaking Bengali. His mother fled their violent family home, leaving him behind, and he was sent to live with his frail grandmother. But as she couldn't even look after herself properly, much less a little boy as well, she handed him over to the state and eventually he ended up in the care of ISSA, Mrs Sood's adoption agency, just as I had. The legal process permitted orphans to live in an ISSA orphanage for two months while attempts were made to restore them to their family or arrange an adoption. Mrs Sood was excited by the idea of placing him with the Brierleys, so we would become brothers.

But Mantosh didn't enjoy the same smooth process of adoption as I had. His was complicated by the fact that he did have parents, even though he couldn't return to them – his mother's whereabouts were unknown and his father didn't want him. With his two months exhausted, he had to be transferred back to Liluah – the intimidating juvenile home I had been sent to – while ISSA continued to try to arrange his adoption by Mum and Dad.

It took two years for the complex legal procedures to be worked through, by which time he'd obviously been scarred terribly by his experiences. The only good to come out of it was that he'd learned more English than I had, which helped him when he arrived in Australia. What happened to Mantosh exposed the harm that the bureaucratic adoption system can do.

*

When Mantosh first arrived, he didn't seem completely sure what adoption meant, or that his move here was permanent. When he began to understand that he wasn't going back to India, he had mixed feelings. I had had similar feelings, but his were far worse, perhaps because of his earlier suffering. When he was young he could become explosively angry without any obvious cause, and though he was a skinny little boy, he could be as strong as a man. I'd never seen anything like it, and unfortunately it made me wary of him when we were young.

Mum and Dad were patient and loving, but firm, and both Mantosh and I think all the more of them for their determination to make a family out of the four of us. It's a brave thing to adopt children, especially from abroad, when the kids you're taking in often come from troubled backgrounds; they can be hard to understand and even harder to help.

Because of the difficulties he was going through, Mantosh required most of our parents' attention. I was reasonably well adjusted by then, but I still needed reassurance that I was loved and cared for. Jealousy of a sibling receiving more attention at home is normal, but Mantosh and I both had fears and insecurities from our pasts that probably made us react more strongly than most.

One night, soon after Mantosh arrived, I ran away from home. It was a measure of how much I'd changed – and how much I'd learned about the resilience and love in a family – that I didn't try living on the streets again. My escapade was much more typical of a Western kid testing his parents' commitment to him: I made it to the local bus depot around the corner, but soon got cold and hungry and went home. Still, although Mantosh and I had our differences, we also went swimming and fishing together, and played cricket and rode our bikes, like any young brothers.

Mantosh didn't enjoy school as much as I did. He was frustrated and disruptive in class, although he at least shared my enthusiasm for sport. He was the target of more racist comments than I was, to which he would retaliate and then find himself in trouble. That seemed to spur on his bullies, who would make a game of stirring him up. Unfortunately, the teachers seemed ill-equipped to assist a boy struggling to adjust to a new way of life. It didn't help that initially

Mantosh wasn't used to accepting direction from women in authority, a prejudice learned from his family in India. I'd had to overcome some of these cultural differences, too. One day my mother was driving me somewhere in the car and heard me say sulkily, 'Lady no drive.' She pulled over and said, 'Lady no drive, boy walk!'

I quickly learned my lesson.

Because Mantosh needed so much of my parents' attention, I was left to my own devices for more of the time than I might have otherwise been. But apart from causing the odd tantrum, it didn't much bother me, perhaps because that's what I was used to in India. I liked my independence. And we still did plenty of things together as a family – we would go to a restaurant every Friday as a family outing, and we took trips away during school holidays.

The World Expo 88, held in Brisbane, was the first event of its kind I had ever been to. I saw Pakistan's tallest man and the unbelievable monorail, which took people to different stations representing areas of the world. Mum and Dad had a two-day family visit pass and it was the most amazing place I had ever seen. I was so excited to go there because of the exposure it gave me to the pavilions of different countries.

I always loved seeing my grandma from my

mother's side. She lived a few hours from Hobart in a place called Burnie that we had to travel to via car. I always felt sad when we had to go back home after a few days. Sometimes my grandma came home with us to mind me during the school holidays while Mum worked at the pharmacy. We would play hide and seek, read books and cook Hungarian doughnuts and poppy seed cake, and Granny would tell me about her life and what she used to do as a teenager with her brothers back in Hungary. Even though I didn't understand much, she always explained things with simplicity and I sort of knew what she meant.

I loved swimming so much, it was an ordeal for my mother to get me out of the water at the pool or the beach. I think that because I was never in a controlled environment while swimming in India I had more confidence in people around me, knowing that if I was ever in trouble someone would rescue me. Dad and I would go to the Lauderdale Beach sailing club every Sunday during the summer and the first thing I would do was get into my swimsuit and go for a swim or paddle on my styrofoam surfboard until it was lunchtime. I'd then head back out until it was time to have dinner, which usually was a barbecue, and to go home. I loved the water, the sun and the sand.

At one point, Mum and Dad planned a major family trip – to travel to India together. At first, I was wildly excited about it, and Mantosh seemed to like the idea too – we'd always been surrounded by Indian things and thought a lot about the country, so we all talked about what we'd see and where we'd go. Of course, neither of us knew where our home towns were, but we'd visit other places and learn more about the country we were from.

As the date of the trip neared, both Mantosh and I began to feel anxious. Most of our memories of India weren't happy ones, and the more real the prospect of going back there became, the more vivid those memories seemed to be. A lot of things that we'd been able to put behind us – or at least put from our minds – began to return as the trip approached. I certainly didn't want to go back to Calcutta, and I began to be agitated that any other place we visited might turn out to be my home, or somewhere I would recognise. I still wanted to find my other mother, but I was happy where I was – I wanted both things, not one or the other. It was confusing and increasingly upsetting. And maybe subconsciously I was worried about getting lost again. I can't imagine what must have been going through Mantosh's mind.

In the end our parents decided that it was better

for the moment to leave things as they were: the trip
would stir up too many dark emotions.

7

Growing up

By the time I began high school, the map of India was still on my wall, but I hardly noticed it next to my posters of the Red Hot Chili Peppers. I was growing up Australian – a proud Tassie boy.

Of course, I hadn't forgotten my past or stopped thinking about my Indian family. I was still determined to remember every detail of my childhood memories, and often went through them in my head, as though telling myself a story. Sometimes I would lie in bed, visualising the streets of my home town, seeing myself walking home through them, opening the door and watching over my mother and Shekila as they slept. I prayed my mother was still alive and well, and my sister and brothers. Transported there in my mind, I would concentrate on sending them a message that

I was okay and they shouldn't worry. It was almost a meditation. But these memories were the background of my life, not the forefront. I dived into my teenage years pretty much as any other kid might.

At high school there were a lot more kids from other ethnic backgrounds than in primary school, particularly Greeks, Chinese and other Indians, so any sense of being different I'd once felt dissolved. I made good friends, joined a school rock band as guitarist, and still played lots of sport, particularly soccer, swimming and athletics. And because the high school was quite small, it helped Mantosh settle down when he arrived the following year.

I remained pretty independent, though, and did my own thing. By the age of fourteen, I was running off to the local pier with my friends to fool around and drink on the sly. I soon had a girlfriend, too. I wouldn't say I was particularly wild, but I was spending more and more time goofing off. It's tempting to blame my childhood and adoption for my behaviour, but frankly I think I just got swept away in the things that most teenagers discover.

I'd never been particularly academic, and my school marks began to suffer because of all the time I spent playing sport and hanging out with my friends. Eventually I came up against the limit of my parents' tolerance. Mum and Dad were determined, hardworking people, and it seemed to them that I was coasting along a little aimlessly. They gave me an ultimatum: leave school before Year 12 and get a job (as Mantosh later chose to do); work hard and get into university; or join the armed forces.

This was a shock. The idea of the military scared me, as my parents had intended. It sounded too much like the institutions that I wanted to put behind me. My parents' ultimatum reminded me of how badly I'd wanted to learn when I was in India. I'd been given a life I couldn't have imagined, and I was certainly enjoying it, but maybe I wasn't making the most of it.

That was incentive enough to knuckle down: from then on I became a model student, shutting myself in my room after school to review the lessons, improving my marks and even lifting myself to the top of some classes. Once I finished school, I chose a three-year accounting diploma at TAFE, as a stepping stone to university. I also got a job in hospitality.

After that initial wake-up call, Mum and Dad didn't pressure me to follow any particular path, and they never made me feel that I owed them anything for adopting me. As long as I was applying myself, they would support my decisions. They would have been pleased to see me finish the diploma, but, instead of going on to university, I found I was enjoying the money and social life of hospitality work so much that I was happy to leave accounting behind. For several years, I combined work and play – I had various jobs in bars, clubs and restaurants around Hobart, and these were good times, twirling bottles like the actors in the film *Cocktail* and promoting band nights. But when I saw my fellow workers getting stuck in the business with no prospects, I knew I wanted more. I decided to get a qualification in hospitality management, and received a scholarship to go to the Australian International Hotel School in Canberra.

It was in there that my mind was unexpectedly turned again to India and I began to think about how I might search for my childhood home.

*

When I moved into a hall of residence at the college in Canberra in 2007, I quickly discovered that not only were there a lot of international students, but that they were mostly Indian. The majority were from Delhi, Mumbai and Kolkata, as they were called by then.

I'd known other Indian kids at high school, but like me they'd grown up in Australia. Getting to know people who'd grown up in India was completely different. They spoke English with me, but Hindi among themselves, the first I'd heard in years. I'd almost completely forgotten my first language – the Indians at high school had only spoken English. For the first time I felt stripped of my Indianness: rather than being the Indian among Australians, I became the Australian among Indians.

I was drawn to them because they were from the same place as me, some of them from the very city in which I'd been lost. They had trodden the same streets and been on the same trains. They welcomed me into their group, and we'd go clubbing together, eat Indian food, take trips to nearby towns or gather at someone's house to watch Hindi masala ('mixed') movies, those wonderful Bollywood blends of action, romance, comedy and drama. They encouraged me to relearn some of my native tongue, and to explore my culture. I also began to learn about the rapid changes that had gone on as India modernised.

In turn, I told them my own story. To talk about my time in the train station to people who knew Kolkata's massive Howrah Station was completely different. They knew that the river next to it was the Hooghly River. They were astonished I'd survived, especially those from Kolkata, who understood something of the life I must have led. And I'm sure it seemed incredible that someone from that background was now at college with them in Canberra.

All this made my past seem much more real. I had always kept my memories fresh by going over them in my head, but I hadn't spoken about them much for a long time. It didn't seem that important anymore. Each time I did I became Saroo-who-used-to-live-on-the-streets-in-Calcutta, rather than just Saroo, and mostly I wanted to be just Saroo.

My story brought out the detective in my Indian friends. The whereabouts of my home town was a mystery they wanted to solve, and they asked me lots of questions about what I could remember. For the first time since I was in Howrah Station, I began to see the possibility of working out where I'd come from. Here was a bunch of people who knew the country well – the adults I'd needed when I was first lost. Maybe they could help me now.

So I tried out my meagre collection of clues on my friends. There was Ginestlay, which might have been the name of my town, or an area or even a street. And then there was the nearby station where I'd boarded the train alone, called something like 'Berampur'.

They thought it was a good start, even though the Kolkata authorities had tried and failed to work out my origins with these fragments. The traumatic experiences I'd had living on the streets seemed to be imprinted on my mind in great detail. But my first big trauma – being trapped alone on a train carrying me far away from home – seemed to have overwhelmed me. I recalled only snapshots of distress. I was hazy about how long I'd been stuck on the train, but certain that I had boarded at night. I thought I had arrived in Kolkata the next day before noon – it was certainly daytime – and I felt that I had probably travelled for between twelve and fifteen hours.

One of my friends, a girl called Amreen, said she would ask her father, who worked for Indian Railways in New Delhi, if he knew of places with the names I remembered, probably about twelve hours away from Kolkata. I was excited and agitated – this was as close as I'd ever been to the help I'd been looking for on the railway platforms twenty years before.

A week later, he responded: he had never heard of Ginestlay, but there was a suburb of Kolkata called Brahmapur, a city called Baharampur in West Bengal, and a city in the state of Orissa, down the east coast, formerly known as Berhampur and now also named Brahmapur. If there was a suburb in Kolkata called Brahmapur, why had no one ever suggested that it might be the place I was searching for?

The second and third places didn't seem likely; they were both too close. The Orissan city was less than ten kilometres from the coast, but I'd never seen the ocean until I flew over it to Australia. How could I have grown up so close to the sea but never seen it? Once I'd gone on a memorable trip to watch the sun set over a lake not far from my home town, but my first sight of the open sea below the plane astonished me.

My friends thought that, based on my appearance, I might come from West Bengal, the state of which Kolkata was the capital. When I was growing up in Hobart, Mum had told me some elderly Indians we met had also thought it likely I came from the east. Could I be remembering the train journey wrongly? Might the time and distance have been exaggerated in the mind of a frightened five-year-old? Little seeds of doubt were being sown in my mind.

*

In addition to the hunches of my friends, I started to use the internet to search for more information. We'd had internet at home since my later years at school, but compared with today, it was much slower, especially before broadband when there was only dial-up. What we call the internet now was only just getting started as 'the web' when I was finishing school. Wikipedia was in its infancy by the time I started college. Today, it's hard to imagine not being able to find information on any topic imaginable, no matter how obscure, but it wasn't long ago that the internet was used mainly by geeks and academics.

When I was at school there was no social media, either. It was much less easy or common to connect with people you didn't already know, even by email. All in all, I hadn't realised that this relatively new invention could help me find my family.

At college, I not only had Indian friends encouraging me to search, I had 24-hour access to the internet and my own computer in my room. So I started searching for any information I could find using various spellings of 'Ginestlay', with no success. The 'Berampur'-type names led nowhere – there were too many possibilities and not enough information to narrow down my search.

I may have begun to doubt my memory for names and the length of my train journey, but I had no doubts about my memories of my family, or the town and the streets I'd walked as a child. I could close my eyes and see clearly the station in Berampur where I climbed aboard the train: the position of the platform, the big pedestrian overpass at one end, and the large water tower high above. I knew that if I could just see any of the places that had been suggested by my friends and the internet, or if I could somehow see what someone thought was my home town, I could tell straight away if it was the one, even though I couldn't be positive about the names.

Maps didn't help. They weren't detailed enough to show small villages, let alone neighbourhoods or the detailed street plans I needed. For a while I even considered flying to West Bengal to search, but how long could I possibly ramble through parts of the country looking for something familiar? The place was enormous. It was like jumping on random trains at Howrah Station.

Then, I became aware of a map that actually *would* allow me to roam across the landscape: Google Earth. With its satellite imaging, anyone can look at the world from above, sweeping across it like an astronaut. You could view whole continents, countries or cities, or search for place names and then zoom in on the spots that interested you, rendered in astonishing detail – up close to the Eiffel Tower, or Ground Zero, or your own house. When I heard what Google Earth could do, my heart raced. Might my childhood home be visible, if I worked out where to look? Google

Earth could have been invented for me – the perfect tool. I got on my computer and began searching.

As I'd never got even a flicker of recognition from anyone about Ginestlay, I thought that the place sounding like Berampur was the best place to start. And if I found it, my home town would be just along the train line. So I searched for places like Berampur and, as always, the results were overwhelming. There were many variations of the name strung across the length and breadth of India: Brahmapur, Baharampur, Berhampur, Berhampore, Birampur, Burumpur, Burhampoor, Brahmpur . . . on and on they went.

I tried searching for the two places Amreen's father had suggested, in West Bengal and Orissa. Slowly but surely, aerial images of each town appeared on the screen – Google Earth worked exactly the way I'd hoped. I should be able to see any landmarks I remembered, and hopefully identify the right place almost as easily as if I were there in a hot air balloon.

None of the train stations in Baharampur in West Bengal had the overpass I remembered, or any place nearby with a name like Ginestlay, either. The place I was looking for had a range of hills nearby, which the train line ran through, and it wasn't so green and lush. The region I came from was a patchwork of farmland around dusty towns.

The city in Orissa, Brahmapur, wasn't right either.

It was disheartening, but I did not give up hope. It was clear that searching for my home was going to be a mammoth task. Google Earth was an incredible tool, but a massive one. Using it to look over great distances would be hugely time-consuming, given the speed of the internet and my computer. So, after the initial excitement, I told myself I was just mucking about. Occasionally I checked out a few places in the north-east around Kolkata, but I didn't find anything familiar.

Eventually, I gave up. I was searching for a needle in a haystack. I was at college to study, and I didn't want to spend all my free time like a hermit at a computer desk. I'd grown up to be Australian, in a loving family. Fate had delivered me from a harsh existence to a comfortable life – perhaps I needed to accept that the past was past.

Perhaps I also wanted to protect my memories – I'd clung to them so tightly, that I was desperate to preserve the kernel of hope they contained. If I went back, searched, and failed to find anything, would that mean I had to give up all hope of ever finding my home and family? If I could find no trace of them, how would I keep holding on to their memory?

I completed my course and moved back to Hobart in 2009, but by then I'd lost interest in the hospitality industry. I asked my parents if I could work in the Brierley family business, and I was excited when they agreed it was a good idea. Mum and Dad's business sells industrial hoses and fittings, valves and pumps, and Dad manages it. He started the business the day I arrived from India – he had to leave my granddad in the brand-new office to answer any calls while he set off to Melbourne with Mum to meet me.

Working with Dad was inspiring. Some of his determination, his focus on success and his work ethic rubbed off on me. He certainly kept me busy, and working together each day brought us closer. Mantosh later joined the business.

Returning to Hobart, working with my family, meeting a new girlfriend, reminded me that tracing my roots was not the most important thing in my life. People who have been adopted, whether or not they ever knew their birth parents, often describe the constant, gnawing feeling of something missing in their life: without a connection, or at least the knowledge of where they are from, they feel incomplete. I didn't feel that. I never forgot my

Indian mother and family – and I never will – but being separated from them didn't prevent me from pursuing a full and happy life. I tried to concentrate again on the life I had, and put thoughts of my Indian home from my mind.

8
The search

My girlfriend and I split up, and I felt bereft and full of regret. I moved back into my parents' home and went through a dark lonely time when I often felt a failure. My parents wondered if they'd see the positive, optimistic person they'd once known.

After a time I moved in with Byron, a friend who introduced me to a new crowd. His kindness and the fresh faces I met really helped pick me up. If family has been the most important thing in my life, friends have not been far behind.

Byron had broadband internet access at home and I had a new, fast laptop. I began to think seriously about my life in India once more. Each failure to find my home chipped away at the certainty of my memories, so there was a lot to lose, but how could I pass up the chance of discovering where I was from, and maybe even finding my mother?

I decided that I'd search whenever I had some time.

I went over what I knew. I came from a place where Muslims and Hindus lived close by, and where Hindi was spoken. That was true of most of India. I recalled all those warm nights outside under the stars, which ruled out the colder regions of the far north. I hadn't lived by the sea, although I may have lived near it. And I hadn't lived in the mountains. My home town had a railway station, and although India was riddled with train lines, they didn't run through every village and town. Some regions were too lush or fertile, or too mountainous.

I thought I could remember enough landmarks and features to recognise my home town if I came across it: the bridge over the river where we played as kids and the nearby dam wall. I knew the layout of the station and how to get from the train station to our house.

I remembered the other station, where I'd boarded the train, fairly well – the one in the town starting with 'B'. I'd been there quite a few times with my brothers, but they'd never let me leave the station, so I knew nothing of the town itself – all I'd ever seen beyond the exit was a sort of small ring road for cars and horse carts and a road beyond it that led into the town. I remembered the station building, and that it only had a couple of tracks; over the other side was a big water tank on a tower. There was also a pedestrian overpass across the tracks. And just before the train pulled into town from the direction of my home, it crossed a small gorge.

So I had some ways of identifying Ginestlay and the 'B' place if I found them. Now I needed a better search method. I knew that train lines linked the 'B' place with Kolkata. If I followed all the train lines out of Kolkata I would eventually find my starting point. And from there, my home town would not be far away. It was an intimidating prospect – there were many, many train lines from Kolkata's Howrah Station, and it was unlikely to be a simple, straight route.

Still, there was a limit to how far I could have travelled in twelve to fifteen hours, the time I estimated I'd spent on the train. That would allow me to rule out any place that was too far away.

It dawned on me that I could turn this into a painstaking, deliberate task that simply required dedication. Something clicked inside. If all it took were time and patience to find home, with the aid of Google Earth's god's-eye view, I would do it.

*

First, I worked on the search zone. How fast could India's diesel trains travel? Would that have changed much in the last thirty years? My Indian friends from college might be able to make a guess, especially Amreen, whose father worked in the railways, so I got in touch with them. They all said seventy or eighty kilometres an hour. I did the calculations and decided that the place I was looking for was around a thousand kilometres along a train line out of Howrah Station.

On Google Earth I drew a circular boundary line a thousand kilometres from Kolkata and saved it for my searches. That meant I would have to search the states of West Bengal, Orissa to the south, Jharkhand, Chhattisgarh and nearly half of the central state of Madhya Pradesh to the west, Bihar and a third of Uttar Pradesh to the north, and most of the north-eastern spur of India, which encircles Bangladesh. (I knew I wasn't from Bangladesh, where people speak Bengali, not Hindi. Besides, the railway line between the two countries had only existed for a few years.)

My search zone covered some 962,300 square kilometres, over a quarter of India's huge landmass. Within it lived 345 million people, and I couldn't help wondering if it would even be possible to find the four members of my family among so many.

Despite the staggering size of the search zone, I felt like I was narrowing things down. Rather than randomly throwing the haystack around to find the needle, I could concentrate on picking through a manageable portion of hay, then set it aside if it proved empty. I planned to work outwards from Kolkata, the only point of the journey I was certain about.

The first time I zoomed in on Howrah Station, looking at the rows of ridged grey platform roofs and all the tracks spilling out of it like the fraying end of a rope, I was taken straight back to the age of five. I was about to embark on a high-tech version of what I'd done in my first week there, randomly taking trains out of the station to see if they'd carry me back home.

I took a deep breath, chose a train line and started scrolling along it.

*

Progress was going to be slow, even with broadband. When I first zoomed out to see how far I'd gone along the track after hours of scrolling and studying the landscape, I was amazed at how little distance I had covered. But I felt certain that I would find what I was looking for so long as I was thorough. Several nights each week I'd search, then before I turned in, I'd mark how far I'd gone on a track and save the search, so I could take up from that point next time.

Sometimes I would catch my breath at the sight of an overpass, or a bridge over a river, only to find something else that didn't fit, such as a chain of lakes nearby. Sometimes I skipped along a bit, but then nervously went back to repeat that section, reminding myself that if I wasn't methodical I could never be sure I'd looked everywhere.

My housemate Byron made sure I went out in the real world, so I didn't become an internet hermit, but weeks and then months passed while I spent hours on the laptop every couple of nights. I ruled out much of the country around Kolkata, despite the hunch of my Indian friends. I was sure I'd come from further away.

After searching for some months I had a lucky find in the real world – Lisa. Lisa became my girlfriend, and in 2010 we moved into a small flat together. Even then, with our relationship in full swing, I was obsessive about my search. I didn't tell many people about it, because I thought they wouldn't understand. And as for my parents, I was worried that if I told them, they might think I was unhappy with the life they'd given me, or the way they'd raised me, and I wasn't.

Working slowly and carefully, I eventually eliminated whole areas of India, finding nothing I recognised in the north-eastern states or Orissa. I started following lines beyond my original thousand-kilometre zone. South beyond Orissa, I eliminated Andhra Pradesh; Jharkhand and Bihar didn't offer up anything promising either, and as I wound up into Uttar Pradesh, I thought I'd keep going to cover most of the state. Eventually states replaced my zone boundary, and I would mark the progress of my search by ruling out state after state.

I was on the laptop seven nights a week unless I had some commitment I couldn't avoid. Sometimes I went out with Lisa, of course, but the moment we got home I was back on the computer. 'You're at it again!' she'd say, looking at me strangely, as though she thought I might be a bit crazy.

'I have to,' I'd reply, 'I'm really sorry!'

Lisa knew she had to let me keep searching until there was nowhere left to search, even though I became more and more distant. I was looking for my home so I could see my Indian family once more and tell them what had happened to me. I needed to understand my past and myself, and to answer all those nagging questions. Lisa understood all this and didn't resent it, even if there were times when she wanted to ban me from staring at the screen for my own sake. Her greatest fear for me was that my search would fail, but I couldn't let myself think about failure.

As 2010 drew to a close the pace of my search increased. We acquired an ADSL 2+ broadband connection, which meant I could refresh images and zoom in and out faster. Still, I had to search carefully and methodically – if I rushed I'd always wonder later if I'd missed anything. Also, I had to try not to bend my memories to fit what I saw.

By early 2011, I was concentrating on India's centre, in Chhattisgarh and Madhya Pradesh. I spent months poring over them, relentlessly, methodically.

There were times when I doubted the sanity of what I was doing. Night after night, with my last reserves of energy and willpower, I sat staring at railway lines, searching for places I might recognise from my five-year-old mind. It was a repetitive, forensic exercise. Sometimes it felt claustrophobic inching along railway lines, unable to be break free, as if the screen were a small window and I was reliving my childhood ordeal on the train.

And then, one night in March at around one in the morning, in just such a mood, I took a wild dive into the haystack in frustration, and changed everything.

9

Finding home

On 31 March 2011, I began to 'travel' a train line, but the countryside looked a bit green for my dusty old town. I'd followed a line to a junction, but then I zoomed out and idly flicked the map along. I wanted a quick look at where the line from the junction went as it headed west. I watched hills, forests and rivers sweep by, until I noticed a large river that fed into what looked like a massive, deep blue lake called Nal Damayanti Sagar. It was surrounded by some lush country and there were mountains to its north. For a while I enjoyed a little exploration, as if I was on a hike on a huge scale. It was getting late, and I'd turn in soon.

I noticed that there didn't seem to be any train lines in this part of the country. Curious, I found myself looking for one. How did the people of this region travel without rail? Then, as the countryside flattened out into farmlands to the west, I finally came across the little blue symbol for a train station. I was somehow reassured to find it, and I checked out the tiny wayside station, just a few buildings to the side of a reasonably major train line with several tracks. Out of habit, I started tracing the route as it wound south-west. I quickly came across another slightly bigger station, again with a platform on only one side of the tracks but with the township spread out on either side. That explained the overpass, and was that . . . was that a water tower just nearby? Holding my breath, I zoomed in for a closer look. Sure enough, it was a municipal water tank just across from the platform, not far from a large pedestrian overpass spanning the railway line. I scrolled over to the town side and saw something incredible – a horseshoe-shaped road around a square immediately outside the station. The ring road I used to be able to see from the platform. Could it be? I zoomed out, and discovered that the train line skimmed the north-west of a really large town. I clicked on the blue train station symbol to reveal its name, and my heart nearly stopped.

Burhanpur!

I didn't recognise the town, but then, I'd never

visited it – I'd never left the platform. I zoomed back in and re-examined the ring road, the water tower, the overpass, and they were all exactly as I remembered them. That meant, not far away, just up the line, I should find my home town, Ginestlay.

Almost afraid to go on, I crept along the train line to the north. When I saw that the track crossed a gorge just on the edge of the built-up area, I was flooded with adrenalin – I remembered in a flash that the train I took with my brothers travelled on a small bridge over a gorge like that, before pulling in to the station. I pushed on more urgently, east then north-east, in moments zooming over seventy kilometres of green farms, some forested hills and small rivers. Then I passed across some dry flat land broken up by a patchwork of irrigated farmland and the occasional small village, before I hit a bridge over a substantial river. I could see the town's outskirts ahead. Below a bridge, dam walls on either side of the river restricted its flow. If this was the right place, this was the river I used to play in, and there should be a bigger concrete dam wall to my right a little further from the bridge.

And there it was, clearly visible in the sunshine of the day the satellite passed overhead and took the picture.

I sat staring at the screen for what seemed like an

eternity. What I was looking at matched the picture in my head exactly. I couldn't think straight, frozen with excitement and terrified to go on.

Finally I forced myself to take the next step, slowly, nervously. If I really was looking at Ginestlay for the first time in twenty-four years, then I should be able to follow the path I remembered from the river back to the train station, only a short way up ahead. I began to trace the course of the path, which wound along beside a tributary stream, left and right, around a field, under a street overpass and then . . . the station. I clicked on the blue symbol and the name came up on the screen: Khandwa Railway Station.

Khandwa? The name meant nothing to me.

My stomach knotted. How could this be? Everything was perfect, all the way from Burhanpur, which surely must be the 'B' town I had tried to remember. But if the bridge and the river were correct, where was Ginestlay?

I tried not to despair. I had spent a lot of time in and around our local train station as a boy, so I checked off what I remembered – the three platforms, the covered pedestrian overpass that connected them, an underpass road beneath the tracks at the northern end. All these features were reasonably common, but not in the precise arrangement I remembered.

It all checked out. I remembered a huge fountain in a park near the underpass and went looking for it. Sure enough, I thought I detected its familiar circular shape – a little indistinct – in a central clearing, surrounded by trees.

From here, I knew the route to where my home should be. I'd gone over and over it in my head since I was a little boy, so that I never forgot it. I followed the road up from the fountain and along the route of the underpass, and then through the streets and alleys I had walked as a child. It was the way I used to imagine myself walking when I lay in bed in Hobart at night, trying to project myself home to let my mother know I was okay. Before I realised, I'd gone far enough, and I was looking down at the neighbourhood I knew as a boy. I was sure of it.

Still, nothing like 'Ginestlay' came up on the map. It was the strangest feeling: part of me knew but part of me doubted. I was sure this was the right place, but for all this time I'd also been sure of the name 'Ginestlay'. 'Khandwa' rang no bells whatsoever.

Maybe Ginestlay was a suburb of Khandwa. That seemed possible. I looked through the maze of alleys where we had lived. When I'd looked at my suburb in Hobart, the image was very clear. This image was a little blurry, but I was sure I could see the little rectangular roof of my childhood home. Of course, I'd never seen the place from above, but the building was the right shape and just where it ought to be. I hovered over the streets for a while, astonished, trying to take it all in, then I couldn't contain my excitement any longer.

'Lisa, I've found my home town! You've gotta come and see this!' It was only then that I realised it was the middle of the night – apart from a short dinner break, I'd been at the computer for over seven hours.

Lisa poked her head around the corner, yawning, in her nightie. It took her a moment to wake up properly, but even half-asleep she could see I was excited. 'Are you sure?' she asked.

'This is it, this is it!' I replied. In that moment I was convinced. 'This is my home town!'

It had taken eight months of intense searching, over the nearly five years since I'd first downloaded Google Earth.

Lisa grinned and hugged me tight. 'That's so great! You did it, Saroo!'

*

After a sleepless night, I went to see Dad at work. For him, the news would come out of the blue. I tried to rehearse what I was going to say, but in the end, I blurted out, 'Dad, I think I've found my home town.'

He turned away from his computer and said, 'Really? On a *map*?' I could tell he was sceptical. 'You're sure?'

I knew Dad was worried that I might get my hopes up only to have them dashed. His caution was understandable, but I needed him to know that I was convinced and I wanted him to be too. Telling Dad somehow made the discovery real. I didn't have any firm plans about what to do next, but sharing the news made me realise that this was just the start, not the end, of a journey. From that moment, it was clear that this was a life-changing discovery, for all of us, even if I found out nothing more.

I was particularly anxious about telling Mum, because she had such a strong belief in adoption and the family it had created. I was worried about how my news would affect her, even upset her.

So that night we gathered at the family home, each of us slightly on edge. I was eager to show them the Google Earth images that had convinced me I'd found my home town, but they responded cautiously. The idea seemed incredible: I'd used a bird's-eye view to search one of the most populated countries on earth, looking for landmarks I remembered from when I was five? And actually found what I was looking for? I showed them the walled dam on the southern edge of Khandwa, the train lines and the underpass I walked through to get to the station, just as I had described it all to Mum when I was little.

At the back of our minds, I think we all wondered what this discovery would mean for the future. Perhaps my parents had always thought this day would come, and feared their son would be reclaimed by India and perhaps lost to them.

Our celebratory dinner was slightly muted, and all of us had lots of questions on our minds.

When I arrived home afterwards, I was full of nervy energy and went straight back to my computer. Maybe there were other ways of confirming what I already knew. I turned to another tool that hadn't been around when I started my search – Facebook. I searched for 'Khandwa', and up came a group called 'Khandwa: My Home Town'. I sent a message to the group administrator:

> can anyone help me, i think I'm from Khandwa. i haven't seen or been back to the place for 24 years. Just wondering if there is a big fountain near the cinema?

The fountain was the most distinct landmark I could remember. The park where it was located was a busy meeting place, and the circular fountain had a statue of a wise man sitting cross-legged. I never knew who he was supposed to be. Some of the town's dreadlocked Hindu holy men – who I now knew were called sadhus – bathed in its cool waters and forbade anyone else from doing so. I remembered once gashing my leg on a barbed wire fence running away from them, after my brothers and I crept into the fountain on a really hot day. My destiny appeared to be riddled with close calls, chance episodes and wonderful, blessed luck. Perhaps my luck would continue.

I went to bed for another restless night.

*

When I woke next day, I opened my computer and saw a response to my query about the fountain on the Khandwa Facebook page:

> well we cant tell u exactly . . . there is a garden near cinema but the fountain is not that much big . . . the cinema is closed for years . . . we will try to update some pics . . . hope u will recollect some thing . . .

It was deflating, and I cursed myself for getting carried away and telling everyone before I was absolutely sure. Later that day, or the next, Mum told me she had looked at the map we'd drawn together in her notebook when I was six, and the position of the bridge, the river and the train station weren't quite what I'd shown her on Google Earth. But was that because I had the wrong place, or because I'd had trouble drawing an accurate map as a six-year-old? She'd also pulled out the wall map I used to have in my bedroom – she kept everything to do with our childhood – and had been surprised to find that it had both Burhanpur and Khandwa marked on it. To her, they seemed so far away from Kolkata that she wondered whether it was possible I'd travelled such a vast distance. It was almost right across the country.

So, my home had been marked on the map above my desk the whole time, if I'd only known where to look. How many times had I stared at all those names? If I had noticed Burhanpur, I'd obviously written it off as being too far from Kolkata. And it *was* much further than I had thought possible. Was it too far? Did the trains go much faster than I'd allowed for? Or had I been on the train for longer than I thought?

The things I'd always been so certain about were dissolving in the face of what I'd found. Would the search erode what I thought I knew and leave me with nothing? It took me a couple of days to think to ask the Khandwa group the obvious question:

> Can anyone tell me, the name of the town or suburb on the top right hand side of Khandwa? I think it starts with G . . . not sure how you spell it, but i think it goes like this (Ginestlay)? The town is Muslim one side and Hindus on the other which was 24 years ago but might be different now.

It took another day to get an answer. But when the answer came it was heartstopping:

> Ganesh Talai

That was as close to my childhood mispronunciation as you could hope for.

*

In my excitement, I called Mum and Dad immediately to tell them that now there could be no doubt: it all lined up. I had found Burhanpur and Khandwa and now, vitally, I had found Ganesh Talai, the area where

I'd lived, where my Indian family might still be living, wondering what had become of me.

I wasn't sure what to do next – it was overwhelming. I kept revisiting the streets of Khandwa on my laptop, searching them for signs, almost paralysed by the prospect of the truth. It was like the time when Mantosh and I were kids, too scared to go to India on the family trip for fear of what we might find.

I tried to convince myself my family couldn't possibly still be there after all this time. How old would my mother be by now? I wasn't sure, but she'd lived a hard life as a labourer, and life expectancy for a woman like her probably wasn't great. Was my sister, Shekila, okay? And Kallu? What had happened to Guddu that night in Burhanpur? Did he blame himself for my getting lost? Would any of them recognise me if we met again? Would I recognise them? How could you possibly find four people in India, even if you knew where they lived a quarter of a century ago? Surely it was impossible. My mind pinged back and forth between hope and fear.

There was only one way to be sure. I had to go to Ganesh Talai and see for myself. And then, if it was my home, I told myself I would be happy just to take off my shoes and feel the earth beneath my feet, and remember the times when I used to walk those streets and paths. I couldn't let myself think further than that, about anyone who might still be living there.

I knew my parents would worry about my going to India. Would it stir up old traumas? And if Ganesh Talai was the wrong place, would I despair entirely? Or would I stay there and search for the right one?

I researched Khandwa, a small regional city in the state of Madhya Pradesh. It had a population about the same size as Hobart's, and Hindu was the main religion. It was a quiet area well known for its cotton, wheat and soybean farming, as well as a major hydro power plant. My family was too poor to be involved in any of that, so all of this was news to me. Like most Indian cities, it's got a long history and a list of Hindu saints attached to it, and it can boast of a writer and a family of Bollywood stars who grew up there. It's not on the tourist trail, but it is on a significant rail junction, where the major east–west line between Mumbai and Kolkata meets another trunk route running from Delhi down to Goa and Kochi. That explains why Khandwa's station is much larger than the one at Burhanpur, although the towns are about the same size.

I watched the few clips of the town on YouTube, but it was hard to tell much from these images. Some footage showed the underpass near the railway station, apparently known as Teen Pulia, and the pedestrian overpass across the tracks, which appeared to have been extended over all three platforms. It still looked like home.

After a few weeks I summoned the courage to talk to Mum and Dad. 'What would you do in my situation?' I asked.

'It's obvious: you have to go,' they said, and Lisa felt the same way. They all wanted to come with me.

I was relieved, and touched, but I needed to go alone. If I was wrong, I didn't want to find out in front of my family, and I also didn't want a group of us descending on Ganesh Talai and making a big scene. Who knew what problems that might cause? I wanted to search for my home quietly and privately.

I could probably have tracked down a phone number for the local police or the hospital in Ganesh Talai and called to ask them about my family or to search for my medical records. I could have provided my family's names, at least, and made some enquiries. It's not a big neighbourhood, and everyone knew everyone. But I feared that word would get out and chancers would start appearing, making false claims. Some might well like the idea of a comparatively well-off prodigal son from the West, and it wouldn't be surprising if a few potential 'mothers' turned up at the station ready to claim their long-lost boy. By the time I got there, I might have made it harder to find the real people I was looking for.

Thankfully, Lisa understood, but my parents were more insistent. Dad promised that they would keep out of the way, or perhaps just he would come and stay in the hotel, then at least he'd be on hand. These were kind and well-meaning offers, but I'd made up my mind.

*

It took eleven months from when I first identified Ganesh Talai to when I eventually boarded the plane to India. Apart from my childhood flight to Australia, it was my first major trip anywhere. There had been problems with my citizenship, which had taken time to sort out, and all the usual travel issues, but the truth is I was putting things off. I was extremely anxious about the trip. I would have to face up to some bad memories returning to India, and I wondered how I'd handle it. I didn't really know if I'd found the right place or whether my family would still be there.

When the day finally came, Mum, Lisa and I had a final cup of coffee together at the airport. I realised, from their advice to me, that I hadn't done such a great job of disguising my anxiety. Then Mum handed me a sheet of photos she'd scanned, showing me as a little boy. It had been twenty-five years since I'd been in India – even my own family might need help recognising me.

I lingered over final goodbyes, feeling sick with nerves. Mum looked anxious, and I suddenly wondered what I was doing. Did I need to find out about the past, when I had people who loved me right here?

Of course the answer was yes. I had to find out where I came from, and at the very least I wanted to see the place I had always dreamed about.

I got on the plane.

10

Meeting my mother

On 11 February 2012, my feet touched the ground in India for the first time since I had left as a child. In the pre-dawn dark I felt a rush of adrenalin as the magnitude of what I was doing hit me.

India didn't exactly welcome me back. I'd landed in the city of Indore, the biggest city in Madhya Pradesh, and my first experiences marked me out as a stranger. I might have come 'home', but this was a foreign country to me. When my bag was not on the luggage carousel, I found I couldn't understand the airport official, who probably answered my questions in Hindi. Not speaking the language of my home felt like being lost all over again, unable to understand what anyone said or to make people understand me.

I struggled past several insistent taxi drivers

offering exorbitant rates for the trip to my hotel and eventually found the courtesy bus. As it pulled out of the airport, the sun blazed down on the confusion of twenty-first century India. At first, much of it looked like the India I had known a quarter of a century earlier. I saw wild black pigs scavenging in side streets, the same sorts of trees on street corners, and the familiar press of people everywhere. The poverty of the place was still plain, but everything looked much dirtier than how I remembered it. People used the roadside as a toilet and rubbish was strewn everywhere – I didn't remember any of this from my own neighbourhood, but maybe I'd become used to the clean, open spaces of Hobart.

When I got out at the hotel, the roar of heavy traffic and the strong smell of sulphur from the drains and sewage hit me. After such a long time, Khandwa would probably seem different too. I slept fitfully for a few hours, then organised a car and driver to take me there the next day.

Khandwa was two hours' drive away, but I paid half the amount the pushy drivers at the airport had asked for the short trip to the hotel. Any sort of street-smarts I had once had were long gone. But perhaps you paid extra for safety: my short, skinny driver took to the roads like a maniac, even by the famously carefree standards of India, which added another shot of adrenalin to my overloaded system. The road from Indore runs through hills and valleys, but I noticed little of the scenery. We stopped occasionally for a chai and I found myself growing more and more anxious about what awaited me in Khandwa.

Under a hot sun in clear skies, we approached the outskirts of town, which had a dusty grey industrial look that I didn't recognise at all. I felt an instant chill. Suddenly, I decided to go straight to the railway station, before the hotel, before anything. That would be the quickest and easiest way to discover whether I was right about this place.

We changed direction. The roads narrowed and traffic slowed to a crawl – it was Sunday and people were out and about everywhere. When I was little, there had been more horses and carts than autorickshaws, but now the streets were clogged with cars and motorbikes.

My mobile phone had a GPS service, which would have laid out a street map for me, but my batteries were low and I wanted my memory to be jolted into action. So I directed the driver from what I could remember, and, sure enough, we found the station where I expected it to be. My spirits lifted.

The station looked a little different from my memories of it, but I instantly had my bearings – from there, I knew the way to anywhere in Khandwa. I knew where I was, and I wasn't far from home.

I felt elated.

Now that I found I was in the right place, I couldn't go any further. Exhaustion overwhelmed me, and I felt like a puppet with the strings cut. Nervous energy had been sustaining me since I arrived in India – and for a long while before that. I asked the driver to take me to the hotel.

As the taxi crawled through the streets, I tested them against my memory. I remembered the place being green with trees everywhere, far less industrialised and polluted, and certainly with no garbage in the streets. The buildings looked much shabbier than I had pictured them. But when we drove through an underpass beneath the train tracks with barely any overhead clearance, memories of just such a claustrophobic road came flooding back. It was surely the one where I had played as a child.

At the Hotel Grand Barrack – as the name suggests, it was once a British Army barracks – I inadvertently offended my driver by offering no *baksheesh* – tip. As an Australian, I simply wasn't used to paying more than the agreed amount, and I'd walked into the hotel before I realised my mistake. I checked in, feeling as if I was a walking culture clash.

Exhausted by my discoveries, and the lengthy trip, I put my suitcase down in my hotel room, switched on the air conditioning and overhead fan, and collapsed on the bed.

But, tired as I was, I couldn't rest. What the heck are you doing? I thought. You've been sitting on planes for an eternity, squashed in a car for two hours more . . . Get going! It was Sunday, two o'clock, and I had come a long way to find my home. I grabbed my daypack and water bottle, and felt a surge of excitement.

Standing outside the hotel, I didn't know which way to go first – roads and lanes led off in every direction – so I retraced the route the car had taken. Soon I was walking on the road parallel to the railway line, striding back towards the centre of town.

The streets were vaguely familiar, but I couldn't quite say that I knew precisely where I was. So much was different, I just couldn't be sure. Doubts began to creep back into my mind. Had I made a mistake? But my feet seemed to know the way, and I walked on, as though I was on automatic pilot. Whether it was jetlag, fatigue or this surreal experience, I felt as if I was looking down on myself as I walked, almost as if I were still using Google Earth. I had failed to take Mum's advice to remain calm and keep my expectations low. Instinct, memory, doubt and excitement were all coursing through me at once.

After a while, I came upon a small green mosque. Baba's mosque – I had forgotten all about it! It hadn't changed that much – it was more rundown and smaller of course – and it was reassuring to find something I recognised. I began to feel again that I was on the right track. But I still relentlessly questioned everything I saw.

Eventually I turned left, and headed towards the centre of Ganesh Talai. It didn't look right at all. There were too many houses – it looked too built up. I began to tremble and my pace slowed. I tried to calm myself down by reminding myself that things change, populations grow – of course it was more crowded. But if old buildings had been knocked down for new ones, maybe my house was gone too! That made me shudder, and I hurried on until I came to a small section of open ground that looked like a spot where I used to play.

I recognised it and yet I didn't. It was the same place, but different. Then I realised what the difference was: the town now had electricity. There were poles and wires everywhere. When I was growing up we had lit our house with candles and cooked on a kerosene stove or with wood. Now that the streets were draped with electricity cables, the whole place looked closed in, busier, different.

I had worked myself up into a state, worrying about what else might have changed. I'd deliberately not allowed myself to think about my mother and my family, and now I was approaching the place where they might still be. Despite my best efforts, all sorts of emotions were bubbling to the surface.

Still I put it off. I decided it was best to start by trying to find my family's first house in the Hindu part of the neighbourhood, before we moved to the Muslim part of town.

Making my way down a street and into a narrow, twisting alleyway, I saw a woman washing clothes. Memories of running around the place flowed through me. I must have been staring, because she spoke to me. A strange man in foreign sportswear, probably rich-looking, I certainly looked out of place. I think she said something like 'Can I help you?' in Hindi, but all I could say was 'No.' I turned and walked on.

After that I couldn't delay the inevitable any longer. Finally it was time to face up to the ultimate point of my journey. It took only a few minutes to walk across the streets that once separated the

Muslim and Hindu areas of the neighbourhood. My heart was in my mouth as I approached the place where I remembered the crumbling brick flat to be. And before I could think about what I was expecting, I found myself standing right in front of it.

It looked so tiny, but it was unmistakable.

It was also unmistakably abandoned. I stood and stared.

*

The rough brick walls were familiar, though the ground level was now plastered with cheap concrete and whitewashed. The doorway to the corner room was in exactly the right place – but the door itself was the size of a window in Australia, and it was broken. I couldn't see much through the cracks in the door, so around the corner I peered in through the sole window, barely thirty centimetres square. I couldn't believe that my mother, sister, brothers and I had occupied the tiny dark space inside. It was perhaps three metres square. The little fireplace was still there, clearly not used for some time, but the clay water tank had gone. The single shelf was hanging off its brackets. Some of the bricks in the outer wall had fallen away, letting in beams of light. The mud, straw and cow-dung floor, which my mother had always swept clean, was now dusty from disuse.

While I looked in, a goat chewed at some hay left on a rock by the door, indifferent to my personal disaster. I'd told myself over and over that I couldn't expect to just fly to India and find my family safe and well in the same place after all this time. Even so, the shock of finding my home with nobody in it was overwhelming. Despite my best efforts, secretly I had been convinced that if I found my way back home, they'd be waiting for me. I watched the goat chew, feeling completely hollowed out with disappointment.

My search was over. What should I do now? I had no idea.

As I stood there, for the first time with no plan in mind, a young Indian woman holding a baby came out of the room next door. She spoke to me in Hindi and I understood she was asking if she could help me. I replied, 'I don't speak Hindi, I speak English.'

'I speak English, a little,' she replied.

I was jolted out of my slump. Quickly, I said, 'This house . . .' and then recited the names of my family: 'Kamla, Guddu, Kallu, Shekila, Saroo.' The woman didn't respond, so I repeated the names and pulled out the sheet of photos Mum had given me before I left. That was when she told me what I couldn't bear to hear: that no one lived there anymore.

Two men walked over to see what was happening. One of them, perhaps in his mid thirties, and with good English, looked at the photos, told me to wait, and then walked off down an alley. I didn't have much time to think about what was happening – other people had begun to gather nearby, curious about what was going on, and about the presence of a foreigner in these streets where tourists were rarely if ever seen.

After a couple of minutes the man returned and said the words I will never forget: 'Come with me. I'm going to take you to your mother.'

He spoke like an official making an announcement, so bluntly that I just accepted it. I didn't absorb what he'd said until I'd begun to follow him down an adjacent alley. Then I got goosebumps and my head began to spin – just moments ago I'd given up after twenty-five years of hoping for exactly this. Could it possibly be true that this passing stranger knew where my mother was? It seemed too unlikely and too fast. After all this time, things were moving at a bewildering pace.

Fifteen metres down the alley, the man stopped in front of three women who were standing outside a doorway, all of them looking in my direction. 'This is your mother,' he said. I was too stunned to ask which one, still half-wondering if it was a prank.

Incapable of doing anything else, I looked from one to the next. The first was certainly not her. There was something familiar about the woman in the middle, and the third woman was a stranger. I looked back at the woman in the middle. Despite the years, I knew the fine bone structure of her face the instant I looked back at her, and in that moment she seemed to know me too. It was my mother.

She was slender and seemed so small, with greying hair pulled back in a bun, wearing a bright-yellow floral dress. We looked at each other for a second longer, and I felt a sharp stab of grief that it took a mother and son so long to recognise each other, and then a rush of joy that we now had. She stepped forward, took my hands and held them, and stared into my face with utter wonderment. I was thinking clearly enough to understand that whatever turmoil I was feeling, at least I'd had some chance to prepare. For my mother, her son had simply reappeared twenty-five years after she had lost him.

*

Before either of us had said a word, my mother led

me by the hand to her house. A long line of people followed, curious to see what was happening. She lived only a hundred metres around the corner. As we walked, she seemed overcome with emotion, speaking to herself in Hindi, and looking up at me again and again, with tears of joy in her eyes.

I was too overwhelmed to speak.

Her house, another conjoined dwelling of crumbling brick, was down a dirt alley, and she bustled me inside and sat me down on her bed in the main room. She remained standing and produced a mobile phone from within the layers of her clothing. When she said, 'Kallu, Shekila . . .' I understood that she was calling my siblings. They were still here too? She spoke excitedly on the phone, shouting and laughing, and calling out, 'Sheru! Sheru!' It took me a moment to realise that my mother was saying my name. Was it possible I'd been mispronouncing my own name all this time?

The little knot of people that had assembled outside was growing rapidly, and soon there was quite a crowd. They were chatting excitedly to each other and into mobile phones – the miracle of the son returned from the dead was clearly big news, and word was spreading fast. The house was soon filled with boisterous, celebrating people, with more crowded in the alley outside the front door and even more gathered on the adjoining street.

Fortunately, some of these well-wishers had a little English, and my mother and I were finally able to talk through translators. The first thing she asked me was, 'Where have you been?' It would be a little while before I could give her a full answer, but I provided a quick outline of how I came to be lost in Kolkata and ended up being adopted in Australia. Not surprisingly, she was astonished.

My mother told me that the man I had spoken to in the street had come to the house she was visiting and simply said to her, 'Sheru is back.' Then he had shown her the sheet of paper with the photographs on it that Mum had given me, which I don't even remember him taking, and said, 'This boy who is now grown into a man is nearby and asking about Kamla, which is you.' That seemed a strange thing to say, but I learned that my mother had converted to Islam many years earlier and had taken the new name Fatima, but I think she will always be Kamla to me.

My mother described her reactions better than I ever could mine: she said she was 'surprised with thunder' that her boy had come back, and that the happiness in her heart was 'as deep as the sea'.

When she had seen the photos she had started

shivering and ran from the house into the alley, where she was joined by the two women she had been visiting, and that was where they had been when I appeared at the top of the alleyway. As I walked towards her she had felt cold and shivery, with 'thunder in her head' as joyful tears welled in her eyes.

I had thunder in my head, too. After the long, slow journey and the highly emotional ups and downs of walking the streets of Ganesh Talai to our old flat, everything was now happening in a mad, chaotic rush. There were people shouting and laughing everywhere, pressing in to get a look at me, a babble of Hindi I couldn't understand, and my mother smiling and crying. It was too much to take in.

Later, I realised that I had been just fifteen metres away from her, literally around the corner, when I turned up in front of our old home, but if that man had not come along and helped me, I might have walked away. I'm haunted by the chance that I might not have found her, that we might have stood so near to each other and never known.

We weren't really able to talk properly, as messages were translated, and people asked questions, and the story was repeated for the benefit of newcomers. My mother would turn to her friends, grinning widely, then simply look at me or hug me with tears in her eyes. Then she'd speak on the phone again for a while, to spread the word.

There were a lot of questions to be answered, of course, and most of them by me. My mother had no idea what had happened to me after that night I disappeared. With so much to tell her, it was slow work, but luckily, after a while, we had the help of an unlikely interpreter, a woman who lived a few doors away, called Cheryl. Her father was British, her mother Indian, and she had somehow found herself living in Ganesh Talai. I was so grateful for Cheryl's help; with it, by degrees, I managed to make myself understood to my mother. Later I would be able to tell her everything, but at that first reunion I could only cut through the chaos with the basics: being trapped on a train, ending up in Calcutta, and being adopted and growing up in Australia. She was astonished that I had come back after so many years; that I'd come from somewhere as far away as Australia was incomprehensible.

Even at this first meeting, she told me she was grateful to the parents who had cared for me in Australia. She said that they had the right to call me their son because they had raised me from a child and made me the man I was today. Her only concern for me, she said, was that I should have the very best life

I could. It was extremely moving to hear her say these words. She wasn't to know it, but they took me back to being a little boy at the Nava Jeevan orphanage, deciding whether to accept the Brierleys' offer of adoption. She allowed me to feel, without reservation, that I'd made the right decision. She also said she was proud of me, which is all anyone can wish to hear from their mother.

When I looked around me, I saw that the rundown building in which she lived was in some ways even more dilapidated than our abandoned home. The bricks in the front wall were crumbling, leaving obvious gaps. In the front room of about two by three metres, where she slept on the single bed on which I was seated, two pieces of corrugated iron channelled rainwater from the roof into a bowl in the small adjacent bathroom, with its squat toilet and tub of water for washing. It disturbed me to see that it was built in a way that meant rain could just blow inside. There was a slightly larger room at the back, serving as a kitchen. But although it was far too small for all the curious people who were trying to squeeze inside, her home was larger than our old place, and at least it had a terrazzo floor rather than compacted dirt. It was in shocking condition, but in the context of Ganesh Talai, it represented a step up, and I knew she would have had to work hard for that. I learned from others that she was too old to carry stones on her head on building sites anymore, and now worked as a house cleaner. Despite the hardness of her life, she told me she was happy.

People kept arriving over the next couple of hours, crowding around the barred window and the doorway, chatting excitedly and being filled in on the gossip. My mother held court for many groups of visitors, sitting next to me and holding my face or hugging me while she talked, or leaping up to take a phone call.

Finally, a young woman arrived, with her husband and two sons, as my mother was holding me and crying. It was Shekila. She burst into tears as I stood to embrace her. Then Kallu arrived and we instantly recognised each other. He'd come alone on a motorbike, and was stunned to lay eyes on me. I knew how he felt. Each of us saw his brother as an adult for the first time. Neither of my siblings had had any cause to learn English, so this was another reunion of tears, smiles and speechless wonder, before some simple communication with Cheryl's assistance. It was bittersweet to be so close to my family and yet still unable to speak freely because of the barrier of language.

Shekila told me that when our mother called her about me, she hadn't believed it – she'd thought it might be someone pulling a scam, or playing a joke. But my mother's conviction, and especially her description of the sheet of photos of me as a kid, persuaded her. She'd thanked God for the miracle and quickly got on a train to join us. When she laid eyes on me again, she had been 'lost in time', taken back to the days when I looked after her. She had known it was me straightaway.

But where was Guddu? Of all the stories I wanted to hear, his was top of the list. What had happened that night in Burhanpur? Was it something he thought about often? Above all, I wanted him to know that I didn't blame him for anything, and now I'd finally found my way back.

That's when I was told the hardest news I've ever heard. I asked my mother about Guddu, and she replied sadly, 'He is no longer.'

Guddu hadn't come home either after that night I was lost. My mother found out a few weeks later that he had died in a train accident. She had lost two sons on the same night.

I couldn't imagine how she had borne it.

If there was anything more I could have wished for from that visit, it was to see Guddu again, just once. It was because I'd missed him so much that I made him take me to Burhanpur. To hear that he had died was devastating.

Later, I learned more about that evening and what my mother thought had happened to us both. At first, she was a little annoyed that I'd gone off with Guddu, because she needed me to look after Shekila. But India then was not like Australia, where a child missing for an hour can cause alarm. My mother was often gone for days, and even young children might be in and out of the house unsupervised. So initially she wasn't too concerned. But after a week had passed, she began to worry. It wasn't unusual for Guddu to be away for weeks, but it was irresponsible of him to keep me away for this long. Kallu hadn't seen us on his travels and didn't know whether we'd been around Burhanpur, and my mother started to fear the worst. She had Kallu ask around Khandwa and Burhanpur if anyone had seen us, but they heard nothing.

Several weeks after our disappearance, a policeman came to the house. More worried about me, being the youngest and least capable, my mother thought he had come with news of where I was, but he hadn't – he had come about Guddu. He said that Guddu had died in a railway accident, and showed her a photo of his body. Guddu was found by the tracks about a kilometre outside Burhanpur, and the policeman was there to ask her to formally identify him. I asked if she had been sure it was him, and she nodded slowly. It was still a very painful subject for her, so I got the rest of the details from Kallu. Guddu, just fourteen, had somehow fallen from a moving train, and either went under a wheel or struck something fixed by the side of the track. It was an unimaginably horrific thing for a mother to have to see.

I wanted to visit Guddu's grave, but my family told me that wasn't possible – houses had been built over his graveyard. The builders hadn't even moved the remains of the dead before they began construction. The owners or developers didn't want to know, or didn't care.

It was hard to hear that my brother had disappeared without a trace.

I felt as if my brother had been taken from me, just as I had been taken from him, and in a corner of my mind I understood a little more of what my family must have felt when I vanished. We didn't even have a photograph of Guddu – we could never afford a family portrait. He had been part of us, as we had been part of him, and now all that remained of Guddu was our memories.

I wasn't sure that my family entirely understood

why I was so upset about not having a grave to sit by. For them it was long in the past, but for me his death had happened that very day. Not being able to grieve for him properly was something I really missed after I returned to Australia. The last thing he had said to me on that platform in Burhanpur was that he would be back. Perhaps he'd never returned; perhaps he'd come back to find me gone. Either way, I'd hoped to be reunited with him. Now I'll never know what happened that night – our mysteries will never be solved.

My family feared I had suffered the same fate, or something even worse. They weren't even sure whether I was alive or dead. I felt for Kallu particularly: he lost two brothers and suddenly became the eldest male in the family, which carried responsibilities in our community. He would have been equally responsible for the family's welfare with my mother, a huge weight on his young shoulders.

I also learned a little about my father. He was still alive, but no longer lived in Khandwa – he'd moved with his second family to Bhopal, the capital of Madhya Pradhesh, a couple of hundred kilometres to the north, the city that was made famous by a chemical disaster at the Union Carbide plant in the early eighties. The family still hated him for abandoning us, so my curiosity about him would have to wait.

Amid all the chaos and celebration that first day, Cheryl told me that some people were asking my mother how she was sure I was her son. Wasn't it possible that I was an imposter, or that we were both mistaken, swept away in events because we so wanted them to be true? My mother answered that a mother knows her child anywhere – she'd had no doubts from the first moment she saw me. But there was one way to be completely sure. She held my head in her hands and tilted it, looking for the scar above my eye from when I fell in the street, running away from a dog. There it was, on the right side, just above the brow. She pointed to it and smiled – I was her son.

*

My mother's house was full of wellwishers late into the evening. Eventually I had to go – I was completely drained, but my head and heart were full to bursting. It took a long while to say goodbye to everyone, even without many words in common: there were lots of long looks and hugs. Perhaps we were all wondering whether, after we parted this time, we'd meet again. I promised that I would return the next day. My mother finally let me go, and watched as I climbed behind

Kallu on his motorbike and sped off. We couldn't talk, but I thanked him as I got off at the Grand Barrack and he left for the hour's ride back to Burhanpur, where he now lived – the town I'd spent so long trying to find.

Back in my room, I thought about how my life had completely changed since I left it, just that afternoon. I had found my family. I was no longer an orphan. And the search that had meant so much to me for so long was over. What would I do now, I wondered.

I thought a lot about Guddu. It was hard to imagine what might have happened to him. It seemed hard to believe he just fell – Guddu was so confident getting on and off trains, he'd worked on them for so long. Could there be another explanation? Perhaps he had returned to the station and gone looking for me. The worst possibility was that he might have felt guilty about leaving me alone, and in his panic to find me had taken risks or been preoccupied, and fallen. He might have assumed I'd gone home, but he never went back to check. It was hard not to think that if I hadn't boarded the train that night, Guddu might have returned as planned and he'd still be alive now.

I knew in my head that I couldn't accept responsibility for his fate, but in my heart it was a dark thought that was hard to shake. And although I usually felt there was an answer for everything, and that you just needed to work at a problem until you solved it, this time I had to accept I could never know the truth of what had happened to my brother.

Before getting into bed, I sent a text to Mum and Dad at home in Hobart:

> The questions I wanted answered have been answered. There are no more dead ends.
> My family is true and genuine, as we are in Australia. My mother has thanked you, Mum and Dad, for bringing me up. My brother and sister and mum understand that you and Dad are my family, and they don't want to intervene in any way. They are happy just knowing that I'm alive, and that's all they want. I hope you know that you guys are first with me, which will never change. Love you.

Not surprisingly, it was hard to sleep.

11

My Australian family

It was the middle of the night when my text reached my parents in Australia. It was very big news, and later they said they felt like they'd won the lottery. The generosity they'd shown offering a home to whichever two children they were sent, now extended to my Indian mother and siblings. Rather than feeling threatened, they were happy for me, and my Indian family, another remarkably selfless act from two remarkable people.

Who those people are, and how they came to adopt me and Mantosh, is part of my story.

*

My Australian mum – Sue – was born on the north-west coast of Tasmania, to parents who had emigrated from central Europe after World War Two. Her mother, Julie – my grandmother – was born in Hungary, in a poor family of fourteen children. Julie's father abandoned his wife and all their children, just like my Indian father. Like my older brothers, Julie's older siblings tried to help out as best they could.

When the war came, most of Julie's brothers were taken away to fight and died in battle. Julie's family fled Hungary, and didn't return – it was too dangerous. As the war drew to an end, Julie was just nineteen years old.

Mum's father, Josef – my grandfather – was Polish and had a traumatic childhood of his own. When he was five years old his mother died and his father took a new wife. His stepmother hated Josef so much it's said she tried to poison him. Eventually he was sent to live with his grandmother. Because of his stepmother, he grew up with a deep bitterness against women.

When Nazi Germany invaded Poland at the start of the war, Josef joined the Resistance and took part in bombing and shooting missions, but became deeply disturbed by what he experienced. Finally, he fled Poland and ended up in Germany, like my grandmother.

Josef was a good-looking man – literally tall, dark

and handsome – and when Julie met him, she fell in love. They married, and had a baby, my aunt Mary. They wanted a fresh start, away from Europe, so they boarded a ship that ended up sailing to Australia.

As soon as they arrived, Josef went to a work camp in Tasmania where he was set to work building houses. For a year or more Julie had to stay at the infamous Victorian migrant camp at Bonegilla, near Albury–Wodonga, taking care of baby Mary. When they were offered a farm to share with another family outside the town of Somerset, near Burnie, Josef and Julie were reunited. Josef worked hard, and before long he bought the farm next door and built their cottage. Mary was six when Mum was born, in 1954. Sixteen months later, she had a younger sister too, called Christine.

Like many survivors of war, Josef was psychologically scarred. His moods swung between depression, rage and violence. He was a big, powerful, frightening man, who came from a background in which beating wives and children was commonplace. Mum's upbringing was very harsh.

Polish to the core, Josef drank a lot of vodka every day, and insisted on traditional meals of pan-fried pork with cabbage and potatoes. Mum hated it, and became an emaciated and unhealthy child.

Josef's building business prospered and he bought a lot of property. Perhaps he was Somerset's first millionaire, although no one is sure exactly how much he was worth. Unfortunately, as his mental health worsened, his business suffered. It led to his downfall and broke up the family.

*

My Australian mum grew up quickly and left school in Year 10, when her father insisted she get a job. She worked in Burnie as a pharmacy assistant, and her wage gave her some independence for the first time in her life. She earned around fifteen dollars a week, two dollars of which she was proud to give her mother for her board. She spent most of the rest on things she might need for married life, which she put in a hope chest.

One day, on a lunch break with a couple of her girlfriends, Mum noticed a young man who was up 'all the way' from Hobart. His name was John Brierley. He later asked the girls about their friend Sue, and not long afterwards he called her and asked her out.

John was a twenty-four-year-old surfie, handsome, blond, tanned, polite and easygoing. His English father was a British Airways pilot who had retired at fifty and emigrated with his family to the warmer climate of Australia. The teenage John hadn't been too sure about leaving England at first, but once he got out to Australia and into the sun and surf, he loved it. Dad hasn't been back to England since.

In 1971, a year after they met, Dad proposed. Mum was only seventeen. They were married on a Saturday, moved to a small flat in Hobart, and Mum started work on the Monday at a pharmacy there. It was as if Dad had turned up on a white horse, swept her off her feet, and carried her away to the city. They worked and saved hard to buy a block of land in the waterside suburb of Tranmere and started building. In 1975 Mum turned twenty-one in her own home.

Though Mum managed to leave Burnie, her family's fortunes worsened, which affected her deeply. Her father ended up in prison, bankrupt, and her mother finally left him. Mum – by this time mother to two adopted sons – asked her to join us in Hobart. Mantosh and I enjoyed having our gran close by. We never met our grandpa, who died when I was twelve.

*

Mum and Dad were attracted to the 'alternative' ideas being discussed in the seventies. People were worried about overpopulation, and the Vietnam War – luckily Dad avoided being sent to fight in Vietnam. Mum realised that one way to make a difference was to adopt children in need from developing countries. Because of her background, Mum had no illusions about traditional families; she and Dad agreed that there were other ways to create a family beyond having children themselves.

As a teenager, Mum had had a strange experience. She'd had a kind of 'vision' of a brown-skinned child standing by her side. She sensed it so keenly she could even feel the child's warmth. It was the first time in her bleak life that she'd experienced an overwhelming feeling of something good, and she held on to it.

As a young married woman, with a like-minded husband, she had the chance to make her vision come true. So, although they could have had children themselves, Mum and Dad agreed that they would adopt children from a poor country, and give them the home and loving family they needed.

*

It wasn't that easy. Under Tasmanian law at the time, couples who could have their own children weren't permitted to adopt. There was also a rule that the younger adopting parent could be no more than forty years older than the child. This rule protected babies and young children from being adopted by elderly people who might struggle to care for them.

Sixteen years passed after their decision to adopt. My parents chose to sponsor needy children overseas (as they still do) and enjoy life, dining out, sailing and taking holidays every year.

Then one day, Mum met a beautiful little brown-skinned girl, Maree, who had been adopted by a local family who also had given birth to a son. Mum realised that meant the law preventing fertile parents from adopting must have changed. She enquired about adoption again, and to her joy she found that she and Dad could now apply to adopt children from overseas.

After many interviews, documents and police checks, they were approved to adopt. Then they had to choose a country to send their file to. They had heard from an adoption group in Victoria that the agency ISSA, in Calcutta, acted faster than other agencies to place needy Indian children in new homes. Mum had always been fascinated by India and knew something about the conditions many Indian people were living under: in 1987 Australia's population was 17 million; in that same year in India, around 14 million children under the age of ten died from illness or starvation. Adopting one child was merely a drop in the ocean, but it was something, and it would make a huge difference to that one child. So they chose India.

Some adoptive parents wait ten years for a child who meets their requirements: they might want a baby to raise from infancy, or only a boy or a girl, or a child of a particular age. Mum and Dad felt it was important to offer help to whoever needed it. So they simply said they wanted 'a child'.

The motto of ISSA, run by the wonderful Mrs Saroj Sood, is: 'Somewhere a child is waiting. Somewhere a family is waiting. We at ISSA bring them together.' In our case it really was as simple as that. Only a few weeks after their application, Mum and Dad received a call to say they had been allocated a child named Saroo, who didn't know his surname or anything else much about his origins. Mum says that from the moment they saw my picture they felt I was theirs. It seemed like fate had required them to wait sixteen years for me to be ready for them.

Mum was delighted when word came through: she'd always felt it was her destiny to have an adopted child by her side. Things happened quickly: only seven months after they applied to adopt, and scarcely three months after their approval, I arrived.

Mum's own terrible childhood made her a terrific mother to the children she adopted, and also an inspiration to us as adults. I love her for the person she is, but above all I respect her for the way she's gone about her life and the decisions she and Dad made. Certainly, I'll always be profoundly grateful, to both my Australian parents, for the life they've given me.

*

Today, Mum wishes more Australians would think about helping children in need, either through sponsorship or adoption. She wants Australia to replace the various state laws on inter-country adoption with one simpler federal law, and believes that if governments made it a little easier, maybe more families would adopt children like me.

12

Feeling at home

The day after I had been reunited with my mother, brother and sister, Kallu picked me up on his motorbike early and took me back to our mother's house. She was almost as excited to see me as she had been the day before; perhaps she really hadn't believed that I would come back.

Kallu had already made the trip from Burhanpur with his wife, son and daughter all balanced on the motorbike, then came to the hotel for me. When we reached the house he presented his family to me. I had been delighted the day before to discover I was an uncle to Shekila's two sons, and I loved meeting my niece and third nephew.

For a brief quiet interlude we had tea, smiling at each other, then the stories began – with help from Cheryl and other translators – and the endless visitors. That was how it was to be for the next four days. Shekila soon joined us with her husband and children, having again made the two-hour journey from her home in Harda, a hundred kilometres to the north-east.

My family were surprised to learn that I had no wife and kids. If I'd grown up in India I suppose by this age I'd have a family too. But they seemed pleased to hear that I had a girlfriend, at least, although I wasn't sure my mother understood the concept.

By that second day, the local news media had heard about the lost boy who had returned as a man to the streets of Ganesh Talai. They were soon joined by the national media, who arrived bristling with TV cameras. Their questioning – mostly through translators – was relentless, and as I told my story over and over again, it began to feel as though it had happened to someone else.

I never imagined that my return would cause such a fuss, and I wasn't ready for it. But I found something wonderful in it. India has more than a billion people, and it can seem a chaotic, even harsh, place. There are kids roaming the streets with no one to care for them, yet here in Ganesh Talai – in fact, around the whole country – people were wildly excited because just one of those lost children had managed to be reunited with his family after so long apart.

As even more people came flocking to see me, the gathering turned into a public celebration, with music and people dancing in the streets. My return seemed to inspire and energise the whole neighbourhood, as though, sometimes, miracles happen.

My family all hold emotions in until they build up such pressure that we have no choice but to release them. When we had some time to ourselves, we all wept a lot, from happiness but also from sadness for the time we'd lost – I was now thirty, Kallu thirty-three and Shekila twenty-seven. I had last seen Shekila as a tiny child whom I'd had to keep watch over, and now she had two beautiful children of her own.

But something good had come out of our tragedy. With Guddu and me gone, our mother had just been able to afford to send Shekila and Kallu to school. Shekila had become a schoolteacher, able to speak and write Hindi and Urdu, but not English.

I remembered something and grabbed a bit of charcoal from the fireplace, showing her. She laughed. When she was only one or two years old, I would sometimes find her eating charcoal, perhaps out of hunger, her little mouth and face blackened. She became addicted to it, with terrible results, but after some special care she recovered, free from any lasting damage. The fact that we could laugh about it now showed how far we had come from those days.

Kallu had also done well for himself. He was now a factory manager who supplemented his wage by working as a school bus driver. So in one generation, my family's occupations went from stone-carrying labourer to teacher and manager. That the remaining children had managed to lift themselves out of poverty was a bittersweet result of the family's loss.

But life hadn't been easy for Kallu – I was deeply saddened to hear that I'd been right about his life after Guddu and I disappeared. The burden of being the only 'man' in the house had weighed on him heavily. Although he had also been sent to school after my disappearance, he had cut his schooling short in order to learn to drive, so he could get better work to help support Shekila and our mother. The pain of loss had never left him, and eventually caused him to move to Burhanpur, leaving not only Ganesh Talai but Khandwa altogether. He told me that he'd even questioned his Hindu faith at times, but had eventually felt that the gods would 'do justice' one day by bringing me back. My return affected him deeply – perhaps it would mean that some of the wounds he had carried for so long could begin to heal, and the burdens be shared.

We talked more about the difficult times my family had endured after my disappearance – Shekila admitted she'd been anxious about sending her little kids to school, in case one day they didn't come back – but there was laughter too. One thing that left me bemused was the discovery that I had been named Sheru, Hindi for 'lion'. I'd mispronounced my name ever since I was lost – and now I'd forever be Saroo.

I found that being in Ganesh Talai brought back a lot of memories about my life there, and talking with my family brought back even more. Many of them I was too young at the time to understand. The things I learned that day, and in the couple of days that followed, helped me to fill in some of the gaps in the picture of my early life – a life that's ordinary for millions of small-town Indians. It also helped me understand the life my birth mother had led, and admire even more her resilience in the face of its harshness.

*

My Indian mother was named Kamla after the Hindu goddess of Creation. I remembered her as a beautiful woman, and I still found her so, despite the passage of so many backbreaking and often heartbreaking years. Her family was of the Rajput warrior caste, and her father was a policeman.

My father was shorter than her, broad-chested, with a square face, and even as a young man his hair was flecked with grey. He always dressed completely in white, in the Muslim custom, and he worked as a building contractor. He was twenty-four and my mother was eighteen when they married.

When I was around three, Guddu nine, Kallu six, and my mother pregnant with Shekila, my father announced he was leaving us to live with a new wife. As a Muslim, he was permitted to take another wife. It was a terrible shock. My father had met his new wife at one of his building sites, where she was a labourer, hefting bricks and stones and carrying them around on a tray on her head.

After my father left us, my mother would still see him at times, where he lived on the town's outskirts. His second wife was very jealous of her and would drive her away, and my mother was convinced it was she who prevented my father from seeing us. I certainly can't remember him visiting us at home.

My mother decided not to divorce my father, although she could have under Islamic law, since he had abandoned her. She remained married to him, even though he no longer lived with her or supported her or their children. When she spoke of that terrible time she described it as a hurricane tearing through her life. Sometimes she was so disorientated that she didn't know where the sky ended and the ground began. She wished to die – she even contemplated giving us all poison, or having us lie down on the nearby railway line to be killed by the first passing train.

It was then that she decided to move us to the Muslim part of Ganesh Talai, to the flat that I found empty when I returned. She felt her Hindu family wouldn't take her back in, but the Muslim community might be supportive. Also, the more prosperous neighbourhood would be a better environment for her children to grow up in.

I don't remember having any religious instruction as a child, although I did occasionally visit the local Muslim shrine kept by Baba. But I do remember my mother telling me one day that I wasn't to play with my friends anymore because they were Hindus. I had to find new – Muslim – friends. These days the religious segregation I remembered has been relaxed, and there are no longer clearly separated Muslim and Hindu areas. Despite our move to the Muslim area, my mother didn't formally convert to Islam until after my disappearance. Even then, she didn't veil her face, as some of her visiting friends did.

The biggest impact Islam had on my upbringing was circumcision. We weren't converts so I don't know why I had to endure it. It was done without anaesthetic, and is still one of my clearest and earliest memories. I was playing outside with some other kids when a boy came up and told me I was needed at home. When I got there, Baba – the Muslim holy man – and some other people had arrived. Baba told me that something important was going to happen, and my mother told me not to worry, everything would be all right. Then several men I recognised from the neighbourhood ushered me into the upstairs room of our building.

There was a big clay pot in the middle of the room and they told me to take my shorts off and sit down on it. Two of them took hold of my arms, and another stood behind me to support my head with his hand. The remaining two men held my body down where I sat on top of the clay pot. I had no idea what was going on, but I managed to stay calm – until another man arrived with a razor blade in his hand. I cried out, but they held me fast as the man deftly sliced. It was very painful, but over in seconds. He bandaged me up and my mother nursed me on a bed. A few minutes later, Kallu went into the upstairs room and the same thing happened to him, but not Guddu. Perhaps he'd already been circumcised.

That night the neighbourhood held a party, with feasting and singing, but Kallu and I could only sit on our rooftop, listening. We weren't allowed to go out for several days. We were forced to fast and wore only a shirt with no trousers, while we recovered.

Without my father's financial support, my mother had to seek work. Soon after the birth of Shekila, she went off to labour on building sites, like my father's new wife. Fortunately, she was a strong woman and able to do the heavy work involved. She worked six days a week for a handful of rupees, carrying heavy rocks and stones on her head in the hot sun from morning until dusk. Her wage was something like a dollar and thirty cents a week. This was standard for rural labour in India at that time. Guddu went to work too, and his first long shift washing dishes in a restaurant earned him less than half a rupee.

Begging for food in the Muslim neighbourhood provided a more varied diet than we'd had before – we occasionally got to eat meat, such as goat and chicken. During festivals or parties, for a marriage or other celebration, we sometimes ate special foods. There was often a festival of some sort going on, which meant we all had some fun and some free food – lots of it.

For clothing, we wore hand-me-downs from neighbours. Luckily, with the warm climate, we didn't need much – simple cotton clothing sufficed. Education was out of the question. The school I used to hang around, watching the lucky students come and go, was Saint Joseph's Convent School, which Khandwa children still attend.

Being the eldest, Guddu felt responsible for our survival, and he was always looking for extra jobs to bring in a little more money. He had been told it was possible to make money hawking things on the platform of the railway station, so he started selling toothbrush and toothpaste packs to travellers. That landed him in jail, under some interpretation of child labour laws. He was known to local police – as were Kallu and I, and many young boys in our neighbourhood – as a chancer, maybe a petty thief. For example, we had worked out how to cut holes in bales of rice or chickpeas stacked at the station for the cargo trains, to collect some food for our table. Generally, we'd get away, or get a clip over the ear. Nobody considered us a great menace to society. But for some reason they kept Guddu in jail, even though the laws were designed to protect him.

After a few days, a local policeman told my mother where he was. She took us all to the juvenile prison, an imposing complex of buildings, and pleaded with the officers until Guddu was released. I have no idea what she said, but it would have been clear she wasn't leaving without her son.

Our father had abandoned us completely, leaving our mother to raise us alone. My family told me that when he did live with us, he could be violent, taking his frustrations out on us. Of course, we were helpless – a lone woman and four small children – against an angry man. He and his new wife wanted to be rid of us, and even tried to force us to leave Khandwa altogether. But my mother had no money to leave, nowhere to live and no other way to survive. Her small web of support didn't extend beyond Ganesh Talai. Eventually, my father and his wife quit the neighbourhood themselves and moved to a village on the outskirts of Khandwa, and our lives improved a bit.

I was too young to understand my parents' separation. My father simply wasn't around. On a few occasions, I was told he'd bought new shoes for all of us – rubber thongs.

I have only one memory of seeing my father. I was four and we all had to go to his house to visit his new baby. It was quite an expedition. My mother got us up and dressed and we walked into the centre of Khandwa in the terrible heat to catch the bus. I kept an eye on Shekila, who soon became exhausted. The bus trip was only a couple of hours, but with the walking and waiting, the journey took all day. There was an hour's walk at the other end, and it was night by the time we reached his village.

We spent the night huddled together in the entranceway of a house. My mother knew the owners, who had no room inside to offer us, but it wasn't unpleasant because the nights were hot, and at least we were off the streets. The next morning, after we had shared a little bread and milk, I found out my mother wasn't coming with us – she was not permitted. So we four children were escorted up the road by a mutual acquaintance of our parents to our father's place.

Despite all this I was very happy to see my father when he greeted us at the door. We went inside and saw his new wife and met their baby. It seemed to me his wife was kind to us – she cooked us a nice dinner and we stayed the night there. But in the middle of the night I was shaken awake by Guddu: he said he and Kallu were sneaking out and asked if I wanted to come along. All I wanted to do was sleep. When

I woke again it was to hear my father answering a loud knocking at the front door. A man had seen my brothers running from the village into the open country beyond. He was worried they could be attacked by wild tigers.

I later learned that Guddu and Kallu were upset by what was happening in our family, and wanted to run away from our father and his other wife. Fortunately, they were found later that morning, safe and sound.

But one problem morphed into another: that same morning, standing in the street with my mother, I saw my father approaching and realised that he was chasing after my mother, with a couple of people following behind him. Not far from me, she suddenly stopped and spun on her heel to face him. They argued, shouting angrily. Quickly they were joined by other people who all took sides. Perhaps their argument tapped into the tension between Hindus and Muslims at the time, because it quickly turned into a confrontation, with the Hindus lining up with my mother, and the Muslims lining up with my father. Tempers were high, and many insults were exchanged. We children gravitated towards our mother, wondering what would happen with all the shouting and jostling. Then, shockingly, my father hurled a small rock that hit my mother on the head.

I was right next to her when it struck her and she fell to her knees, her head bleeding. Luckily, though, this act of violence seemed to shock the crowd, cooling tempers rather than exciting them. As we tended to my mother, the crowd on both sides started to drift away.

A Hindu family found the room to take us in for a few days while my mother rested. They told us later that a police officer had taken my father away and locked him up in the cells at the village police station for a day or two.

This episode stayed with me as an example of my mother's courage in turning to face down her pursuers, but also of the vulnerability of the poor in India. Really, it was just luck that the crowds backed off. My mother – and perhaps her children – could easily have been killed.

*

Reminiscing with my family, it was inevitable that the subject of my father would come up. My brother and sister were both completely unforgiving of him. They were sure he would have seen the publicity surrounding my return, but were adamant they'd turn him away if he appeared, however contrite he was. He had abandoned us when we were children and needed his help, and they felt he had to live with the decision he'd made. They also blamed him for the loss of Guddu – if our father hadn't left us, Guddu wouldn't have been forced into his dangerous work on the railways. In their view, the lines of fate went back from Guddu's death and my disappearance to the day that my father brought his new woman into our home and presented her to our then-pregnant mother.

But although my family had sworn they would never have anything to do with him again, no matter what the circumstances, I couldn't feel the same. If he regretted his behaviour, then I could forgive him. I could imagine that he might have made a bad decision, and everything else had rolled on from that. I'd also made a decision that spiralled out of my control, and I couldn't hate him for making mistakes.

Perhaps because I'd been away for so long, I was open to the idea of seeing my father again. It might be hard to imagine why, with so few memories of him and none very favourable, but he is a part of my identity, part of the story of my life. He remained my father, even if I didn't really know him, and I couldn't help but feel that my reunion with my past was incomplete without him playing a part.

I always doubted he would be interested in seeing me, but towards the end of my stay, I received word from someone who knew him. He had indeed heard the reports of my return and was angry that no one in the family had contacted him. He had recently been unwell and wanted to see me. Despite the tone of the message, I couldn't entirely harden my heart against him in his illness. However, there wasn't time to go to Bhopal, let alone raise the question with the family and seek their blessing. I knew I'd have to raise the subject carefully, when we knew each other better. One day I might be able to tell them what I believed, that sometimes families ought to offer forgiveness to people who did the wrong thing in the past.

*

As I spent more time with my family and reconnected with the place I'd been born, I thought about the word everyone kept using, including me – 'home'. Was that where I was, finally? I didn't know.

After I was lost, I'd been lucky enough to be adopted by a loving family. Not only had I lived somewhere else, but I'd become someone else from the person I might have been had I stayed in India. I didn't just live in Australia; I was an Australian. I had a family home with the Brierleys and had made my own home in Hobart with my girlfriend Lisa. I knew I belonged there, and that I was loved.

But finding Khandwa and my Indian family also felt like coming home. Something about being in the place just felt right. I was loved here too, and belonged, in a way I'd not thought about much beforehand and found hard to explain. This was where I'd spent my first years, where my blood was.

So when it was time for me to return to Hobart – a time that came around far too quickly – I deeply felt the wrench of leaving. I promised my mother, sister and brother, and their young families, that I would be back soon. I had come to see that I had two homes, each with their own emotional connections, even if they were thousands of kilometres apart.

13

Returning

I hadn't imagined anything much beyond finding my home and, maybe, my mother. It had seemed like the end of the story, but it was more like a new beginning. I now had two families, and I had to work out how I fitted in to both of them – across the world and across cultures.

My parents and Lisa were relieved to have me back. Even though we'd spoken on the phone every day I was in India, they'd worried I wasn't telling them everything. At first, they'd thought I might disappear again. Then Lisa kept worrying about my safety – I was in one of the poorer parts of a strange country, and who knew what might happen? I began to realise how nerve-racking it had been for them.

Everyone was anxious to hear the details of my

meeting with my family – what stories we had told each other, what the others had remembered of my childhood that I didn't, whether I wanted to return. Looking at their faces, I realised that they didn't know if I still wanted to be here, or was thinking of moving back to India. I reassured them: I was still the same Saroo, although the experience had changed me in important ways. It took me a while to feel like my old self again, though, and to look at Hobart through my old eyes, rather than those of a poor Indian person.

But one thing about me had changed, and it quickly became apparent: I was now someone with a story to tell, and lots of people wanted to hear it. The Hobart newspaper *The Mercury* contacted me soon after I returned. A reporter had got wind of the story somehow and I agreed to be interviewed about it. That opened the floodgates. Next came *The Age* in Melbourne and the *Sydney Morning Herald*, then the international media.

We weren't prepared for my newfound celebrity – perhaps nobody can be. Sometimes the phone rang in the middle of the night as reporters called up from all over the world. I realised I needed help dealing with this attention and got a manager. Soon, book publishers and film producers were calling with offers. It was surreal. I'd never gone looking for fame – I only went looking for my home town and my family! Fortunately, Lisa and my parents were very supportive and gave me all the time I needed. And even though it was exhausting to go over my story again and again with the media, I thought I had a kind of duty to do it. Perhaps it might help and inspire people.

I stayed in touch with my Indian family using online video conferencing. Friends offered them the use of a computer at their house. They didn't have a video camera at their end, so I couldn't see them, but they could see me, and we could talk, either in our stilted way or through a translator. I decided I'd have to set up my Indian mother so that we could stay in touch and see each other from across the world. Now that the family had finally been reunited, I wanted to play a proper part in it, strengthening our bonds, and helping to look after my mother and my niece and nephews.

My journey to find out who I was, wasn't finished. I had some answers – lots of answers – but I also had a lot more questions. One thing was obvious: the trip between India and Australia – between my homes – was one I was destined to make many times.

*

It was almost winter when I went back to India a second time, although the weather was still warm and the air was a choking smog. With weather like this, the sky turns an orange-grey and it doesn't change much as day turns to night. There were still many things I wanted to know and I hoped they would become clearer during my second visit.

I was heading to Khandwa in time for the end of Diwali, the Hindu 'Festival of Lights'. I had forgotten nearly everything about Indian culture, but Indians love festive occasions so I knew it would be colourful and enjoyable. Diwali is a celebration of all things good and a rejection of evil. Lakshmi, the goddess of prosperity, is called on and praised, and families display their wealth before her image in their household shrine, and give thanks for it. There's feasting and gift-giving, and traditionally little oil lamps are lit throughout people's homes, and buildings are covered with coloured lights, like Australia Christmas decorations. There are also a lot of firecrackers, and I heard loud bangs all day, as people let them off to drive away evil spirits. At night, the sky was lit up by fireworks.

I arrived as evening was settling, and reached the narrow streets of the old part of town as the festivities were in full swing. I had dropped my bags at the Hotel

Grand Barrack and then had the taxi driver take me to join my mother and my family in Ganesh Talai. As a Westerner now, I wanted space and certain amenities that her tiny flat couldn't provide, so even though she'd offered to share her place with me, I chose to stay in a hotel and visit her each day.

We drove through the railway underpass, the streets alive with people out shopping, and the driver dropped me off in the square near Ganesh Talai's temple and mosque – located tolerantly close to each other. I set off on foot down the alleys of my childhood, feeling a little more at home.

I had been trying to learn Hindi before I returned and I'd made some progress, but once I was in any sort of conversation, I was all at sea.

My mother greeted me with warmth and joy. Shekila and Kallu had travelled from their homes again so we could all be together, and I was welcomed back into the family without reserve.

My mother had been very accepting of my 'other life', especially considering she had no real knowledge of Australia – other than through cricket. There had been a one-day series on between Australia, India and Sri Lanka at the time of my first visit, and my mother said that after I'd left, whenever she saw cricket telecasts from Australia, she would reach out to the screen, hoping I was in the part of the crowd her fingers touched.

Now she insisted that, as her guests, we all sat in her plastic chairs while she sat on the floor at my feet. We didn't need too many words to communicate how pleased we were to see each other, but it was terrific when Cheryl arrived to translate for us once more.

Still, talking was slow work. Often I would ask a simple question, and then everyone would talk among themselves in Hindi for what felt like five minutes before I got an answer back, usually just a single sentence. I guess Cheryl had to summarise. She was a very generous, patient woman with a keen sense of humour, which was just as well, as my mother, Shekila and Kallu all liked to joke around: it seems to be a family trait.

A woman called Swarnima, who spoke perfect English, was so interested in my life story that she offered to come and translate for us for a while. When I offered to pay her for her time, she explained it was an offer of friendship, not a business transaction. I was overwhelmed by her kindness, and we became good friends.

Over several days, we all spent afternoons in my mother's front room, talking, drinking chai and eating, usually in the company of relatives and friends, with Swarnima translating over the noise of the rusty little fan in the old bamboo rafters of the roof. My mother kept trying to feed me, even though twenty-six years of an Australian diet had certainly fixed any undernourishment I had suffered as a child.

The taste of her goat curries is one of my strongest memories from my early years in Ganesh Talai. I have eaten goat curry in many places, from wayside cafes to upmarket restaurants, but I've never tasted any as good as the one my mother cooks over her little stove in the back room of her home. The balance of spices and the consistency of the meat is perfect – if goat is not cooked correctly, the fibres stick to your teeth. On my first visit, she gave me the recipe, and I've used it to cook a lot of goat curries at home in Tasmania, but hers is always the best.

*

During this visit I learned that my family had never given up on the possibility that I might come back. My mother had seen Guddu's body and mourned for him, but she didn't mourn for me because she couldn't quite believe I was dead. She never stopped praying for my return, and visited many priests and religious leaders in the community, asking for help and guidance. They always told her I was healthy, happy, and in good circumstances, and, amazingly, when she asked where I was, they would point a finger to the south and say, 'He's in that direction.'

My family did what they could to find me, but it was an impossible task. They had no idea where I could have gone. My mother spent every spare bit of money on looking for me – paying people to search, and even occasionally travelling herself around the area, from town to town, asking for any word. Kallu said they had talked a lot with police in Burhanpur and Khandwa, and that he had worked extra time to earn more money to help fund the family's searches. They never learned anything: I had simply vanished.

Even if they could have raised the money to have 'child missing' posters printed, there weren't any photos of me. Praying was all they could do.

I began to realise that just as my search for my mother had in some ways shaped my life, her faith that I was alive had shaped hers. She couldn't search, but she did the next best thing: she stayed near the place where she'd last seen me. That way, if I ever came back, I could find her. Had she moved further away, to live with either of her children, I would have had no chance of tracking them down. The strength of her belief seems to me now one of the most incredible aspects of the whole story.

I've had so many strange experiences and there have been so many amazing coincidences that I've learned to just accept them – even to be grateful for them. Right from the start in Hobart, each night before I went to sleep, I used to imagine my family in India. I would think about the good times we had shared together, and try to send my mother messages that I was all right and thinking of her and the family, hoping that they were still alive and well. Kallu and Shekila told me they had also always treasured their memories of all the fun and mischief of our earliest years – playing together outside or sharing a bath as children. Could a strong emotional bond create a kind of telepathic connection? It sounds far-fetched, but I've been through so much that defies reason that I can't entirely dismiss the idea. It seems to me that somehow the message was received.

Finally, my mother told me that one day she was praying to Allah for blessings on her family when an image of me appeared in her mind. The very next day, I walked back into Ganesh Talai, and into her life.

*

My brother and sister were both married and had

children, but my mother said her only desire was that I married before she died, or, as she put it, before she 'saw the road to God'. She wanted me to have someone to take care of me in this world before she left it. She told me that because of all the publicity, many families would wish for their daughters to marry me, but that any decision about marriage would be my decision and mine alone. I tried again to explain that Lisa and I were very happy together, even though we didn't have any immediate plans to marry. She looked a little sceptical.

Both Kallu and Shekila said they would like to visit Australia one day, although my mother felt the journey was beyond her. Shekila said she didn't need to see kangaroos or the Sydney Opera House, but she did want to see the house in which I was raised. They wanted to meet my Australian family, and told me they prayed for them every day.

One of the most touching things my mother said to me was that if I ever wanted to come back to live in India she would build me a home and go out and work hard so that I could be happy. Of course, I wanted to give *her* a home and do everything I could to make her happy.

*

Money can be a tricky subject in families, but I wanted to share the good fortune I'd had. By the standards of my Indian family, I was a wealthy man, with an annual salary they could only dream of. But I was aware that I had to tread carefully, because I didn't want the issue of money to complicate or taint our new relationship.

The four of us discussed how I could best help. My mother's new work as a house cleaner earned about 1200 rupees a month ($23.50), a much greater sum than she'd earned when I was little, but still a pittance, even in regional India, where the minimum wage is roughly four times as much. We worked out a way for me to supplement her income. When I told my siblings I wanted to buy my mother a house, we discussed whether she might leave Ganesh Talai, and live closer to Shekila or Kallu. But she was happy where she was, and wanted to stay in the neighbourhood she had lived in all her life. So we resolved to find her something there, possibly even the place she was in now, but with much-needed repairs.

There was one more thing I felt I had to do before I could put to rest some of the ghosts of my past. I wanted to go back to Kolkata as an adult, and to get there I would have to take a train from Burhanpur, just as I'd done as a trapped, panicking five-year-old, and see what memories it brought back. With the help of my new friend Rochak – a local lawyer and administrator of the Facebook group 'Khandwa: My Home Town' – I secured a car and driver to take me on the hour and a half trip to Burhanpur, where I was to stay the night before embarking on a journey with painful memories.

I had a train to catch.

14

Kolkata train

In India, there is no such thing as simply booking a train ticket. You need to go to a great deal of trouble to ensure that when you get on that train there is no one already sitting in your seat and that it is yours for the entire journey. This is made all the more difficult when you don't speak Hindi and you don't really know where you're going. I needed some help to work out which train I'd taken across the country when I was a small boy. Swarnima offered that help.

Trains only go north-east or south-west out of Burhanpur, but both directions provided a possible route to Kolkata. One involved going south to Bhusawal, then changing trains and heading roughly east across the country. The other meant heading north-east before eventually arcing south-east without changing trains.

Confronted with these two routes, I had to face up to the fact that my memories had clearly been wrong about one important detail. I had always thought I had woken up on the train and arrived in Kolkata the next day, having travelled roughly twelve to fifteen hours. That was what I'd always told everyone, and it was the basis for a lot of my searching on Google. Now I discovered that there was simply no way to get from Burhanpur to Kolkata in that time. It's a 1680-kilometre rail journey on the northerly route, and only a hundred kilometres less to go east via Bhusawal. My trip was going to take up to twenty-nine hours. I knew I got on the train in Burhanpur during the night, so I must have spent another night travelling. Maybe I slept through the entire second night. Or perhaps, I just lost track of how long it had been. I was a terrified five-year-old, waking and sleeping between fits of panic and crying, with no watch and no way to mark the passing of time. Either way, it was clearly a longer journey than I had remembered. It explained why my meticulous search on Google Earth had failed for so long. I had had no idea back then just how far I had travelled.

I had always been certain that after Guddu and I had jumped off our train, I had slept on a bench, woken up to find a train in front of me and boarded it, all without moving from the platform. We'd travelled south from Khandwa to Burhanpur, so any train on the same line would almost certainly have also been heading south, and you can't get to Kolkata that way without changing trains. I had to concede that either I was wrong about not moving from the platform where Guddu left me – in which case I might well have boarded a northbound train and been spirited directly to Kolkata – or I went south and at some point changed trains.

I couldn't know for certain if I was retracing my trip exactly, but the point was to travel the distance and get a sense of the immensity of the journey. I also hoped to shake loose some more buried memories or put other things to rest. With that in mind, I thought I'd stick with my main memory of being trapped aboard for the whole trip and take the most direct, north-easterly path. It was also the easiest to organise and the most comfortable: there was a service that left Burhanpur at dawn – the Kolkata Mail – which had plied the same route in the eighties, when it was known as the Calcutta Mail. It started in Mumbai, on India's west coast, and reached Burhanpur at 5.20 a.m., which is why I needed to be there overnight. It was scheduled to stop at Burhanpur Station for just two minutes, during which time a conductor would check off the names of the new passengers. How could I have jumped on and fallen asleep before it left the station? And I know there was no conductor around back then; indeed it's a mystery how I didn't see one during my entire ordeal. Conductors are common on interstate trains. When I was trying to find my way back, I always avoided conductors, and probably unwittingly boarded only local trains. They were one of the reasons I couldn't get far out of Kolkata. Now I realise that, had I succeeded in leaving Kolkata, it's likely that, rather than being taken to my home state of Madhya Pradesh, I would have ended up somewhere else again. I could have been doubly, then triply lost. Outside Kolkata, I was unlikely to have been found by an adoption agency.

With the help of Rochak and Swarnima, everything was arranged. When the car to Burhanpur arrived, I set off for a final visit to my mother. Cheryl was able to help translate our last conversation over a parting cup of chai. We posed for family photographs together, which show the striking family resemblance between my mother, my siblings and me.

My mother and Cheryl came out to the car, past a crowd of curious locals who'd gathered to watch the lost boy take leave of his family again. We were re-enacting the day I got lost, so it was an especially wrenching departure. The last time I'd left on this particular journey, as a child, I hadn't said goodbye; now, a quarter of a century later, my mother hugged me tightly, smiling all the while. Although it must have been as emotional for her as it was for me – even more so – this time she wasn't worried that I wouldn't return. She knew that now we would always find each other.

*

I spent the evening in the courtyard restaurant of my hotel in Burhanpur, watching the last skyrockets of people's Diwali stockpiles light up the sky. I knew taking the Kolkata Mail wouldn't solve all the mysteries of my original journey, but it might solve some. I was nervous about the trip, and about what other memories it might challenge – memories that had been the cornerstone of my identity.

I barely slept, so the cooler air before sunrise helped keep me awake. From the autorickshaw that the hotel had booked for me, I saw silhouettes of cows sleeping under awnings and pigs huddled together.

Outside the station, a few people sat around in groups and others slept on the ground. Inside, a brightly lit red sign told me the train was an hour late, so I had ample time to look around the station from which my first journey to Kolkata had begun. It seemed much the same as I remembered it, but some things had changed. I remembered platform benches with wooden slats, including the one I slept on that night. Now the seats were of polished granite within a wooden frame. I remembered Burhanpur station being dirty and full of litter whereas now it was very clean. On the wall there was a poster of a police officer nabbing a man spitting on the platform.

Looking across to the opposite platform, I felt sure it was the one that I'd boarded from, trying to find Guddu. Surely I must have travelled south initially. A chai man plying his trade on the other platform noticed me and I waved to him that, yes, I'd welcome a cup. He gestured at me to stay where I was, then jumped down and crossed the tracks, balancing my cup on his metal tray. Just as he'd clambered back onto his platform, a freight train came thundering through the station – an awesome, frightening spectacle. In Australia trains usually slow down at stations, but here, massive trains hurtled through at regular intervals, shaking the platform. The chai man lived with these trains and his judgement and timing were perfect, but how much harder it would be to make those judgements if you were distracted by grief or guilt. I couldn't help imagining what would happen if you made a mistake. Was that what had happened to Guddu?

Despite the confusion about which platform I'd boarded from and whether or not I'd changed trains, I still have clear, if disjointed, images in my head of the train journey itself: clambering aboard and looking for Guddu, then curling up on one of the seats and going back to sleep; wakening to bright daylight in an empty carriage, hurtling along. I have a memory of the train stopping at least once along its route, with no one around, but of my never being able to open any of the doors to the outside. I'd been confused and frightened, so I suppose it's not surprising I didn't keep good track of time. It must have felt like an eternity.

*

By small degrees daylight came, and people kept arriving – it seemed that the train's late arrival was predictable. Some were wrapped up, for in such a hot place, the dawn cool could be uncomfortable. They carried all manner of suitcases, bags, bundles, and domestic appliances taped up tightly in cardboard cartons. As the light strengthened I saw the big water tower behind the station, which had helped me identify Burhanpur from the sky. I was lucky it hadn't been knocked down or moved, or I wouldn't have recognised the place.

The Kolkata Mail slipped into the station as dawn arrived. It had already travelled 500 kilometres in eight hours north-east from Mumbai, on the Arabian Sea. I stood at the point at which my assigned carriage was to draw up and, sure enough, a conductor consulted his list before ushering me onto the carriage, where I found my allocated seat. I'd booked a 'first-class compartment', which I hoped would be like Agatha Christie's Orient Express, but it fell a little short. There were no luxury carriages on this train, or staff in starched white uniforms with gold buttons offering gin and tonics on silver trays. The worn maroon leather seats were quite hard, but at least for the time being I had the area to myself. The trip wouldn't be as difficult as it had been the first time around, and fortunately I wouldn't have to sit for the whole journey – my ticket included one of the bench bunks across the aisle.

Another mystery from my first journey is that my carriage was empty from the first time I woke until it arrived in Kolkata. An empty train carriage in India is unheard of, yet I am certain it was. I would surely have asked anyone who got on for help, even a conductor. Did I somehow end up on a works train, not meant for passengers, and not a scheduled service at all? If so, why would it have gone all the way to Kolkata?

As the train started to inch away from the platform, I shivered, remembering how this moment had begun the process of my getting hopelessly lost. But I was here to confront the fear I'd felt back then by making the journey again as an adult. I was also returning to Kolkata, to see again the places where I'd survived on the streets. I also wanted to visit Mrs Sood and the others at Nava Jeevan, the place where my fortunes had taken a dramatic turn.

Indian trains aren't terribly fast. I learned that this one averaged fifty to sixty kilometres an hour. My Indian college friends had overestimated typical train speeds, which was lucky. Had they known how slow the trains were, it might have taken me longer to get around to searching further afield. I settled back in my seat, with nearly thirty hours of travel ahead of me.

At first, most of my fellow passengers kept to their cabin bunks, catching up on sleep. But eventually I heard people moving around and murmuring, before they drew back the curtains to reveal families waking up and facing the day.

We had travelled for just over an hour when I had a poignant realisation. If I had travelled this north-eastern route as a child, I would have passed through my home town, Khandwa. Rolling into town just as it was coming to life for the day inevitably made me wonder if I'd done this before, as a sleeping five-year-old. If I had awakened there, I might well have had the opportunity to get off the train and simply walk home, presuming Guddu had met some friends or found something he needed to do. I could have climbed into my own bed, feeling nothing more than disappointment that I hadn't been able to stay away with him for longer. And then none of the things that followed – my experiences on the streets of Kolkata, my rescue and my adoption – would have happened. I would not be Australian, and you would not be reading my story. Instead, perhaps I slept through a two-minute stop at Khandwa, not far from where my mother and sister were probably asleep themselves, and was borne away to a very different life.

The day got underway and the sounds on the train became louder, everyone raising their voice to be heard over the rumbling and clattering of the train on the tracks. Mobile phones blared with ringtones of popular songs from Hindi films, and in the background was what sounded like a compilation CD of different styles of contemporary Hindi music, including jazz and what seemed to be Hindi yodelling. Wallahs began their regular trips up and down the carriage, selling food and drink with a sort of chant: 'Chai, chai, brek-fist, brek-fist, om-lit, om-lit.'

Stretching my legs on a little walk, I found the pantry car, where cooks stripped to the waist fried huge quantities of chickpea and lentil snacks in smoking oil, and boiled mountains of sliced potato in vast vats. The vats and pots rested on bricks and were heated by enormous jets of gas, and the cooks tended them with long wooden paddles. It was amazing to watch them do all this on a bumpy train.

I didn't see any carriages on the Kolkata Mail like the one I'd been trapped in, with barred windows and rows of hard wooden benches. On that train you couldn't walk between the carriages – the doors only opened onto the platform. It seemed more and more likely that on my first trip, I'd been in some sort of carriage that wasn't in use – the bustle and noise of an Indian train are inescapable, and there was no chance that the carriage would otherwise have remained empty.

As we travelled north-east, the landscape we passed through was as I remembered it: flat, dusty and seemingly endless, although this time I was calm enough to take in some of the details of the place: expanses of cotton and wheat fields, irrigated crops and chilli plants so laden with fruit that they looked red from a distance, as well as the usual cows, goats, donkeys, horses, pigs and dogs. Combine harvesters worked side by side with bullocks and carts bringing in the crops, while some farmers harvested by hand, building piles of hay. There were villages of tiny brick and plaster houses painted in pastel colours – pale pink, lime green and faded sky blue – and roofed with old terracotta tiles that looked like they could fall off at any moment. We also passed through tiny railway stations painted in the brick-red, yellow and white patterns of Indian Railways. I must have seen a few of these when I hurtled along back then, praying the train would stop at one. I wondered whether anyone in these fields had looked up at a passing train and seen a small face at the window, gazing out in fright.

I thought about Kolkata, and found that I was more excited than anxious about this visit. Even though parts of it would be full of memories, I was looking forward to seeing how much it had changed.

Night had begun to descend, and it was dark by the time I'd folded the seat down and unpacked the Indian Railways linen from its paper covering. I lay down on my bunk, and found I could still see out the window to watch bicycle lights, house and temple lights flash by as the train rolled on.

With the train's bumping and swaying, an unexpected sense of wellbeing came over me. I felt at ease lying there, bouncing along in my bunk amid the chatter of people speaking in languages that sounded familiar but which I didn't understand. During the day, I'd had a chat with a curious little boy from the next open compartment. He was about ten years old and keen to try out his school English, with 'What's your name?' and 'Where are you from?' He seemed to be able to tell that I was not from India, despite my looks – maybe it was my clothes, or that I didn't join in conversations in Hindi or Bengali. When I told him I was from Australia, he mentioned the cricketer Shane Warne. After talking about cricket for a bit, he asked me, 'Are you married?' When I said I wasn't, he told me how disappointed he was for me. 'Who are your family?' he asked next, and I found myself hesitating. 'My family live in Tasmania, but I also have family here, in Khandwa, in Madhya Pradesh,' I said at last. That seemed to satisfy him, and I realised that it had also begun to satisfy me.

*

Late in the morning of the next day, we began to approach Kolkata. From the train, I could watch how the tracks we were on merged with many others, so there came to be numerous sets of rails in parallel, running into Howrah Station. I might have travelled these lines as a boy, but who knows? I might not have managed to get on any that came out to this western edge of the city. There seemed to be a vast number of lines, which could take a person in every possible direction. Now I saw that I'd never stood a chance of finding my way back home by train.

We passed through level crossings where trucks and cars and autorickshaws waited, with everyone blasting their horns. It wasn't long before we were deep in one of the world's biggest cities, along with somewhere between 15 and 20 million other people. It was 12.20 p.m., exactly thirty hours after my departure from Burhanpur, when the train coasted into the massive, red-brick Howrah Railway Station, which gave me tingles of recognition as we inched up to the platform and stopped.

I had returned.

When I got off the train, I took a minute or two to simply stand in the middle of the busy station concourse and let the crowd rush by me, just as I had back then. This time people surged around me, as they would any adult standing in their way, whereas last time I'd stood here, pleading for help, I don't think they even saw me. In a crowd this size, everyone was anonymous, invisible. Who would notice one frightened kid?

The station building itself was hauntingly familiar. I'd begged in it, slept in and around it, and spent those weeks making futile train trips to try to get out of it. It had been my home at a most traumatic time of my life. But now it was just a train station, albeit a very big one, and busier than any I'd ever seen.

I didn't notice any homeless children inside – perhaps they were more likely to be moved on these days – but I did see a couple of small groups once I walked outside the building into the brutally strong sun. They had that unmistakable look about them: grubby from street living, and somehow both idle and alive to opportunities, such as someone passing close by from whom they might beg or perhaps steal. Could I have ever found myself a gang, or had I been too wary or naïve? It's hard to imagine I could have survived the streets on my own for much longer than I did. I would have become one of these kids, or died. Visiting Howrah Station again brought back memories of the time when I was scared and crying and needed salvation and solace. I wished someone had helped me at this place, but no one did. When I saw the homeless children and families I couldn't just walk past and ignore them, so I offered money and food. Life works in mysterious ways. The good fortune I have needs to be repaid to those less fortunate and the balance restored.

I found a taxi. Before long, I was heading to the hotel my travel agent had booked, which turned out to be quite upmarket, with Indian and Western food, bars, a gym and an infinity pool. I went for a swim: at the pool you could lounge around on recliner chairs on the pool deck, or swim over to the infinity edge and look out at Kolkata, many floors down and extending as far as the eye could see, along with its smog, traffic chaos and poverty.

*

One of the main reasons I'd come to Kolkata was to meet the woman who'd played a vital part in my life. Mrs Saroj Sood was not only still alive, but still working for ISSA, and I'd arranged to visit her in her office. I linked up with my Bengali translator and took a taxi through the mad traffic, dust and stink of untreated sewage.

The ISSA office was in a rundown Victorian

building in Kolkata's Park Street quarter, an area with many restaurants and bars, and the Flurys tearoom, which people visit for the famous cucumber sandwiches and cake. The place looked exactly as it had twenty-five years before.

Mrs Sood, now in her eighties, was surrounded by official-looking files in a cramped inner office, an old air conditioner stuck hazardously onto the wall above her. Her eyes widened when I walked in and introduced myself. We shook hands and embraced. 'I remember your mischievous grin. Your face has not changed,' she told me, in her excellent English, smiling widely. We had last seen each other in Hobart, a few years after my adoption, when she had arrived escorting another adoptee.

She asked me about both of my mothers and then sent someone to find my adoption file. I looked at the pin-up boards on the walls, covered with pictures of smiling children. Mrs Sood had been working to help needy children in this same office for thirty-seven years. In that time, she had arranged adoptions for around 2000 Indian children, some to families in India and others to families overseas. She also had a daughter of her own, a successful businesswoman who often told people that she had 'donated her mother' to the work of adoption.

Born in Delhi, Mrs Sood gained a law degree and became interested in adoption. She arranged her first adoption within India in 1963, and three years later helped a Swedish exchange student, Madeleine Kats, to adopt an Indian girl in Sweden. Kats became a journalist, and when she wrote of her experience, mentioning Mrs Sood, other people from abroad started asking for help to arrange an adoption. And so it all began.

Mrs Sood was trained by the Missionaries of Charity, the order that Mother Teresa founded; she was even blessed by Mother Teresa, who was later to be named a saint by the Catholic Church. With her supporters, she registered ISSA in 1975. Seven years later, ISSA set up the orphanage I stayed in, Nava Jeevan, meaning 'new life'.

Mrs Sood told me that my adoption had gone through smoothly, especially compared to international adoptions today. Now, a central authority manages intercountry adoption, but it is more complicated and commonly takes a year, and sometimes as long as five years, for everything to be finalised. I could feel her frustration, and I knew that Mum felt the same way – she had become a passionate advocate for making international adoption easier, after going through long delays in adopting Mantosh, and seeing how staying longer in care had affected him.

In 1987, it was simpler. Mum and Dad were approved for adoption and met an ISSA staff member bringing adoptees to Australia, who showed them my file. They immediately agreed they would take me. Two weeks later Mrs Sood visited them herself, on a trip to escort Abdul and Musa from Nava Jeevan to Australia, and brought back the photo book my new parents had prepared for me.

While we drank tea together, my file was brought and I was able to see my actual adoption documents. The pages were faded and looked fragile, as if they could fall apart at a touch. A photograph of me in Australia, which my parents had sent after I arrived, was attached to the file. I was grinning and holding a golf club, standing in front of an old-fashioned golf buggy. There was also a photocopy of my passport, with a photograph of the six-year-old me looking steadily into the camera. My official documents and passport all had my name as 'Saru', which is how it had been recorded since I arrived in the police station. It was Mum and Dad who had decided on the more anglicised spelling, 'Saroo'.

The file revealed that I had come to the attention of the authorities in Calcutta after officers at

Ultadanga Police Station had taken me into custody on 21 April 1987. I was assessed and taken to Liluah, the juvenile home, where I was classified as a child in need of care. There were two other categories for children at Liluah – those whose parents had come to the attention of the police and courts, and those who themselves had committed offences – and we were all lumped in together.

I had been in Liluah for one month before a hearing in the Juvenile Court on 22 May had given me into the care of ISSA. The agency was given two months to find a child's family and reunite them or to have an orphaned child declared 'free' to be adopted into a new family. If unsuccessful, the child would have to return and remain in Liluah, although ISSA could continue to pursue their case. This was Mantosh's fate: it took ISSA two years to untangle the difficulties within his family and have him released for adoption.

In my case, staff at ISSA took a photo of me – the first I'd ever had taken – and had it published on 11 June in a Bengali daily newspaper with a notification that I was a lost child. On 19 June they published it in a newspaper in the state of Orissa (now known as Odisha), because they thought I might have boarded the train in the coastal city of Brahmapur. Of course, there was no response – it was on the other side of India from where I actually lived. I was therefore officially declared a 'neglected child' and was formally made 'free' for adoption, after my agreement, on 26 June.

My case for adoption by the Brierleys came up for hearing on 24 August and was approved – so I was in Nava Jeevan for two months. I was issued with a passport on 14 September, departed India on 24 September and arrived in Melbourne on 28 September 1987. From the moment the teenager with the handcart had taken me into the police station until the moment I stepped off the aircraft in Melbourne, the entire process had taken only a little over five months. Mrs Sood said that if I was being adopted now, the process would take years.

Nobody at ISSA knew that I'd spent some weeks on the streets of Kolkata. Confused and no doubt a little frightened about what was happening to me, I'd just answered the questions that were put to me. And even if they'd asked me directly about it, I probably wouldn't have been able to tell them much – I was poor and uneducated, and my language was too limited to be able to speak convincingly. ISSA had only learned that I'd been on the streets years later, when Mum told them after she'd learned about it from me. Mrs

Sood said they had been astounded. Most couldn't imagine a five-year-old from a small town surviving on the streets of Kolkata alone for a few days, let alone several weeks. I had been incredibly lucky.

After Mrs Sood and I had said our fond goodbyes, and I'd thanked her again for everything she'd done for me, a driver took me to a quiet residential street of apartment blocks in the northern suburbs, looking for Nava Jeevan. In fact, the orphanage had moved, and the building I knew was now used as a free daycare centre for children of poor working mothers.

At first I was convinced we'd come to the wrong place, but when I went into the downstairs quarters, I found the Nava Jeevan I remembered. There were a dozen or so young children taking their afternoon nap, stretched out on mats on the floor. These kids, though, were collected by their mother and taken home at the end of the day.

Two more places remained for me to visit. Firstly, we went to the Juvenile Court in which I was pronounced an orphan, then to Liluah Home. My time there had not been happy, which I think was why I'd left it till last.

We crossed the landmark Howrah Bridge and went past Howrah Station, threading our way through narrow alleyways to reach the imposing building, which looked almost like a fortress. As the car pulled up outside, I saw again the massive red rusted gates that I had never forgotten, with the small hatchway entrance to one side, just like a prison. The gate was immense in my childhood memory, and was still imposing now. The high brick walls were topped with metal spikes and jagged glass.

Now, as the blue sign over the entrance informed me, it had become a Home for Girls and Women. Boys were sent elsewhere. Although it looked the same, and there were still guards on duty outside, it felt a little less brutal somehow – perhaps it was just that this time I was here as a visitor.

Inside, we came across a large pond that I barely remembered being there. The buildings appeared smaller and much less menacing than they had. But something about the atmosphere still made it feel like a place you would want to get out of as soon as possible.

I never imagined when I left here that I would one day willingly return, yet here I was now, looking over the place, a tourist of my old terrors. I saw the same kinds of bunk-lined halls in which I had slept and dreamed of release. More than any other visit I made, Liluah put the pain of my past somewhat to rest at last. After all, what alternatives did the authorities have in dealing with lost and abandoned children? They put them somewhere they tried to make safe, and gave them food and shelter while they searched for a place for them. These homes weren't set up to make kids' lives miserable, or to allow adults to prey on them. But when you put that many kids together, some of them much older than others and some of them violent, bullying is inevitable and abuse is possible, even likely.

I felt thankful that I had survived relatively unscathed.

*

On my final day in Kolkata I returned to the streets near Howrah Station, and the little group of cheap cafes and shops that still clung to the top of the banks of the Hooghly River. It was still a place for poor and homeless people, there was still no sanitation, and a lot of people lived in makeshift lean-tos. I walked around the stalls, recalling how I used to smell the mouth-watering fruits and fried foods on sale here, and marvelled that I had been able to detect them at all over the stench of human waste mingled with diesel and petrol fumes, and smoke from cooking fires.

I walked down to look at the river's edge, but the area between the shops and the water seemed to have been divided up into private housing plots. Just as I was trying to work out a way through, several mangy-looking dogs came up a little alley, nosing past my legs, and I decided not to put my anti-rabies shot to the test. Instead, I took the footpath to the impressive steel span of the Howrah Bridge, and before long joined the stream of people at the start of its pedestrian walkway, which links the city of Howrah with central Kolkata. When I first crossed it, I was escaping from the men from the railway shack. Now I knew the bridge was a major Kolkata landmark, probably the best known in the city. It was one of the last major British projects before India achieved independence in 1947.

The massed humanity crossing it, and the stream of vehicles of all kinds, were incredible. People pushed behind me and rushed towards me. Bearers moved to and from the railway station like trails of ants, with astonishingly bulky loads balanced on their heads. Beggars lined the railing along the walkway, raising their steel bowls and shortened limbs, and adding their chants to the racket around them. The bridge seemed to be a neighbourhood in itself.

Soon the crowds started to make me feel

insignificant, as though I didn't exist. How small I must have felt when I crossed it as a little kid. The traffic noise was tremendous and clouds of blue smoke momentarily cloaked the scene. Breathing in this kind of pollution, day in, day out, must shorten people's lives.

Around a third of the way across the bridge, I stopped at the railing and looked back at the riverbank, to a place below the station and the shops, the area where I had somehow survived as a boy. Now there was a ferry jetty in the place I remembered walking along, and underneath the bridge the bank had been concreted. I couldn't see if the sadhus might still sleep there. They'd felt like guardians to me when I'd slept near them or their shrines.

I looked down at the stone steps – the *ghats* – that led into the powerful tidal waters of the Hooghly, at the place where I had almost drowned, twice, and thought about the man who had plucked me from the water both times. He would almost certainly be dead by now. But, like the teenager who later took me to the police station, he had given me another chance to live. He hadn't profited from his act in any way – unless he was a believer in karma – and I had never thanked him. I was too embarrassed and frightened by the attention when he pulled me out the second time. So as I stood there at the railing looking down at my past, I thanked that man, and then I thanked him again, as the sun began to set and my last day in Kolkata ended in a smoky, pink-grey haze.

It was time to go home.

Epilogue

I had always wanted to bring my two families together, and all of them looked forward to such a meeting. The idea of filming the meeting of my two mothers was suggested by the TV program *60 Minutes*, who wanted to feature it as the centrepiece of a story about my experiences. I worried that my Australian mum – Sue – might feel somehow less bonded to me when she met Kamla, the woman who had given birth to me, who I had called Maa as a child. Would Kamla find it impossible to connect with Sue, or feel awkward about their meeting in front of cameras? I knew Sue was nervous about that, as well as about her first visit to India.

Despite my concerns, everyone agreed, although my dad was unable to join us this time. For now, it was to be my mothers laying eyes on each other for the first time.

When my two mothers first met in Ganesh Talai, with the *60 Minutes* crew filming, time seemed to stand still. All concerns washed away as I watched my mothers – who had given me not just one life, but two – embracing with tears in their eyes.

We talked through a translator, but the joy and love we shared didn't need much translation.

Sue greatly admired Kamla's strength and the way she had survived the many challenges of her life.

*

Now, it gives me great pleasure to be able to help my mother in India however I can. I take care of her rent and her food, and whatever makes things more comfortable for her. Typically, she resists, insisting that all she cares about is having me back in her life. I have dual citizenship, which permits me to buy property within India, and despite her soft protests, I plan to buy her a better home in Ganesh Talai, near her friends. Patience is required when doing business in a poor village, and I'm waiting on the paperwork, but Kallu, Shekila and I have found Kamla a place just around the corner from where she waited for me all those years. We all look forward to helping her move into her own home – her first.

I also help another incredibly important woman in my life, without whom I would be unlikely to be here to write my story: Saroj Sood. I am assisting with repairs to the Nava Jeevan orphanage for abandoned babies and lost children. Words can't properly express my gratitude to Mrs Sood and her dedicated staff at ISSA. I will do everything I can to help her help children like me.

*

I have grown up and spent almost all of my life in Australia, and I have family bonds here that cannot be broken. I wanted to know where I came from – to be able to look at a map and point to the place where I was born – and to discover what I could about my past. Most of all, though I hardly dared hope, I wanted to find my Indian family so they would know what had happened to me. My bonds with them can never be broken, either, and I am deeply grateful that I now have them in my life.

I am not confused about who I am or where I call home. I now have two families, not two identities. I am Saroo Brierley.

Revisiting India and seeing the lives of my siblings and my mother has enriched me culturally as well as personally. I look at my brother and sister and admire their traditional focus on family and relationships. It is difficult to put into words, but I feel that perhaps there is something in the West we have lost in our impersonal suburbs and our emphasis on individualism. I am not a religious person, but I am keen to learn more about the customs and beliefs of my Indian family, and to see if they offer some guidance for me.

I am also delighted to know my niece and nephews, and I look forward to being a part of their lives and providing them with whatever opportunities I can.

Had I not become lost, my life would have been hugely different. Much suffering would have been avoided. My family would not have endured the heartbreak of a missing son, on top of the tragic death of another, and I would not have known the pain of separation, and the cold fear that struck me in the train or on the Kolkata streets. But my experiences have undoubtedly shaped me, providing me with an unshakeable faith in the importance of family – however it is formed – a belief in the goodness of people and of the importance of grasping opportunities when they are presented. I wouldn't wish to erase any of that. It's true, too, that my Indian family has opportunities they would not have had if none of this had happened. I feel a strong sense of destiny about these events, intertwining my two families, with me as the linchpin.

I know my mum and dad wouldn't wish for their lives to have been different, without me and Mantosh. I cannot express how grateful I am to them for the love – and the life – they have given me, and I have nothing but admiration for their commitment to helping others less fortunate. I am confident that finding my Indian home will bring my Australian family closer together, rather than making anyone question our connection.

When I told Mantosh that I had found my family, he was very happy for me. Some news of his sadly fractured family has filtered through to us from ISSA and Mantosh has been encouraged by my successful reunion with my Indian family. Despite the painful memories of his childhood, and his struggles growing up, he wishes to reconnect with his Indian mother. We're not sure if it is possible, but I would like nothing more than to see my brother achieve some of the peace of mind granted to me.

I was also delighted to celebrate my good fortune with Asra, my friend since our time together at Nava Jeevan and our astonishing journey to Australia. There are some aspects of my experiences that only Asra and I can share, and I consider myself lucky to have such a friend.

I don't have any regrets about how things worked out, with the exception of my brother's tragic death. I am astonished at the miraculous turns in my story – my Australian mum's vision that led her to intercountry adoption, my Indian mother praying and seeing an image of me the day before we were reunited. Even the remarkable coincidence of finding myself at school in a place called Howrah. It is sometimes difficult not to imagine some forces at work that are beyond my understanding. I don't have any urge to convert that into religious belief. Yet I feel strongly that in my life – from being a little lost boy with no family to a man with two – everything was meant to happen just the way it did.

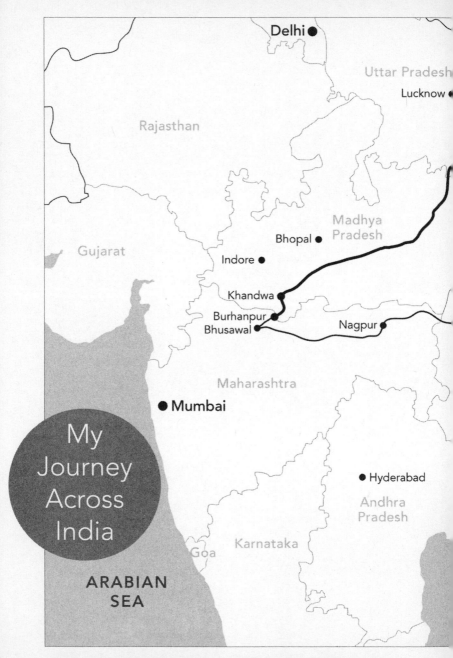

The two most likely rail routes from Burhanpur to Kolkata (assuming only one train change, or perhaps none), although I will never know for certain which was the one I was taken on as a child. No one suspected

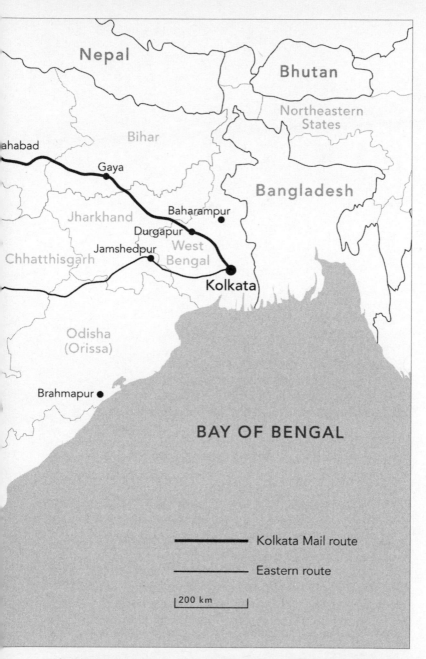

I had been transported so far, which hindered all efforts to find my home and family. In 2012, I rode the Kolkata Mail, crossing the country in much greater comfort.

Behind the scenes of **LION**

Q & A with Saroo Brierley

How does it feel to have a movie made about your life?

I feel proud and touched that there are people out there who are enthralled by my life story, so much so that they would like to make a movie from it. I never thought that something like this would ever happen to me, but I'm happy, and I hope people find that the story resonates with them in some positive way.

How did the movie come about?

Rights to my story were optioned to different production companies over several months – my manager took control of this in the final stages of optioning. The production company whose present-ation was the best won the contract and then acquired the rights to make a live-motion picture film out of my life.

How long did the movie take to be made?
The movie was in production for two years, which in the industry is a pretty quick turnaround time.

Where was the movie filmed?
The movie was filmed in India (Khandwa and Kolkata) and Australia (Melbourne and Hobart).

How was the cast chosen?
The cast were chosen based on their likeness to the people in my life, but most importantly, the quality of their acting.

Did you visit the set? What was a day on set like?
I had the opportunity to visit a set in Kolkata. Due to the amount of people involved, the first take took much longer than I imagined. The location was on the banks near the bridge on the Hooghly River where I escaped to after my frightening encounters there.

ଛଅ ବର୍ଷର ବାଳକ

ସାଦୁ

ଏ ପିଲାଟି ଟୁଟୁପୁରର । ଏହା ବିଷୟରେ ଯଦି କେହି ଜାଣିଥାନ୍ତି ଦୟାକରି ନିମ୍ନ ଠିକଣାରେ ଯୋଗାଯୋଗ କରନ୍ତୁ ।
Indian Society for Sponsorship and Adoption
1 KYD Street, Calcutta.
S/2675

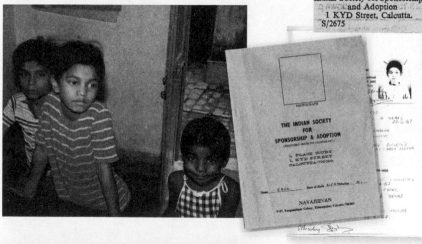

PHOTOGRAPH

THE INDIAN SOCIETY
FOR
SPONSORSHIP & ADOPTION

1 KYD STREET
CALCUTTA-700 016

NAVAJEEVAN

After being picked up off the streets of Kolkata in 1987, I spent two months at the Nava Jeevan orphanage, run by the Indian Society for Sponsorship and Adoption (ISSA). I'm in the middle (above, left), and with my friend Asra standing beside me on the caged front porch (left). ISSA ran lost notices in newspapers (top, right), unaware my home was much farther away than where they were trying.

The photo book prepared by my new parents, the Brierleys, which I was shown at Nava Jeevan to familiarise myself with them and my new home.

FOR SAROO,
NAVA JEEVAN
P.57, RANGANATHPUR COLONY
THAKURPUKUR, CALCUTTA

THIS PLANE WILL BRING
YOU TO AUSTRALIA

THIS IS THE HOUSE
THAT WILL BE OUR HOME
AND HOW YOUR FATHER
WILL WELCOME YOU

THIS IS THE CITY
WHERE WE LIVE —

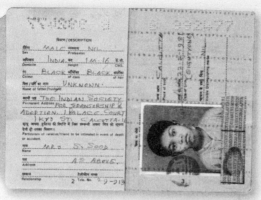

With a passport featuring an invented birthday of 22 May 1981, I left for Australia with other adoptees and official escorts, including ISSA's Saroj Sood, sitting with Asra and me on her lap. It was my first experience of the eye-opening luxury of hotels.

I arrived in Melbourne's Tullamarine Airport in my Tasmania T-shirt and proceeded with the escorts and other children to a VIP room, where our new parents were waiting. Mum and Dad welcomed me with a book and a koala bear. I'm still holding the remains of the chocolate bar we were given on the plane – my first word to my new parents was 'Cadbury'.

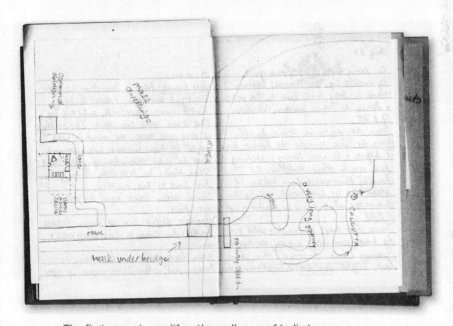

The first maps in my life – the wall map of India I grew up with in my room (seen here as it was prepared for my arrival), and the map of my home town my mother drew with me in her notebook, when at age seven I first told her the story of how I became lost.

I had a happy life growing up in Hobart with my new family, which soon included my younger adopted brother, Mantosh. Above, he sits at the computer next to my friend and fellow Nava Jeevan adoptee, Asra, who occasionally visited from Victoria. Like many teenagers, I had rock star ambitions.

The toy car I chose in Bombay before my flight to Australia and my first meeting with the Brierleys, and the Ganesh necklace I was given when I first arrived in Nava Jeevan.

Google Earth, Image © 2013 DigitalGlobe

Google Earth, Image © 2013 DigitalGlobe

I didn't know the name of my childhood home town. But several years at the computer, searching with Google Earth, led to my incredible discoveries: first, Burhanpur Railway Station (above) – with its familiar water tower – from which I accidentally boarded the train that took me across the country; and then, up the line, the familiar layout of my home town itself (left).

From the satellite view of my search, to returning to India to retrace my steps on the ground: the dam by the rail bridge on the southern outskirts of my home town (opposite, top left); the park fountain, the rail underpass and the railway station (opposite); and the now-abandoned home in which I grew up, in the town's poor neighbourhood (above). Today, I dwarf the front door.

My mother, Kamla, and I were reunited after twenty-six years,
at her modest dwelling (opposite, bottom) just around the
corner from where we used to live. She had remained in the
neighbourhood in the hope I might one day return.

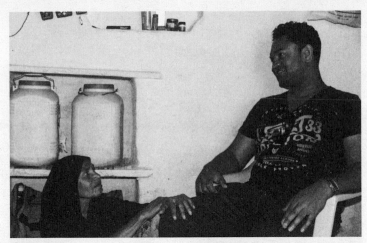

Reuniting with my family was an overwhelming experience. My older brother, Kallu, and younger sister, Shekila, returned home to meet me, although tragically I would discover we couldn't be joined by my oldest brother, Guddu.

© Ssongee Yang and Henry Chen

The train carriage I was trapped on was something like the one above and left – although in those days, the benches on second-class carriages were wooden and not cushioned. I will never be exactly certain of the route I was taken on across India from Burhanpur to Kolkata, but I made the journey again, as an adult with a first-class ticket (top).

In Kolkata, I found Saroj Sood (seated far left) in the same ISSA office from which she'd arranged my adoption a quarter of a century ago. My ISSA file notes: 'We consulted Saru if he would like us to look for a new family for him, and to this he agreed readily.' In the next room (above, right), new orphans napped on floor mats.

It was all too easy to see how a small child was ignored inside the huge and busy Howrah Station (top). Above and left are the imposing walls and iron gates of the Liluah juvenile home, where I was originally sent after being picked up off the streets. Now a home for women and girls only, I wasn't permitted to take photographs inside.

© Nathan Harrison

In my first weeks on the streets, I never strayed far from the distinctive red block of Howrah Station, seen from Howrah Bridge (top). The bridge is a monumental structure, which loomed over me when I survived weeks living on or around the banks of the Hooghly River.

My two families, which make me feel doubly blessed. (Top) Dad and Mum (John and Sue Brierley) and my brother Mantosh. (Bottom) Rear, from left: my brother Kallu and his wife Nasim, their daughter Norin, my mother Kamla and sister Shekila. Front, from left: Shekila's son Ayan, and Kallu's sons Shail and Sameer.

ACKNOWLEDGEMENTS

I offer my deep gratitude to both my families for allowing me to tell their stories as part of mine, and for their openhearted support and assistance in the production of this book. I also thank Lisa for her love and patience during the process.

I am indebted to Saroj Sood for her contribution to my life as well as her help with the book, and to Soumeta Medhora. I would also like to thank Cheryl and Rochak for the help they provided, and especially Swarnima for being so giving of her time and for her friendship.

Finally, I would like to thank Andrew Fraser at Sunstar Entertainment for his guidance, Larry Buttrose, and Ben Ball and Michael Nolan at Penguin.